Top Notes

George Orwell's

Nineteen Eighty-Four

Study notes for Common Module:
Texts and Human Experiences 2019–2023 HSC

Bruce Pattinson and
Michael & Nicola Pitt

———A———
FIVE SENSES
PUBLICATION

Five Senses Education Pty Ltd
2/195 Prospect Highway
Seven Hills 2147
New South Wales
Australia

Pattinson, Bruce and Pitt, Michael & Nicola
Top Notes – Nineteen Eighty-Four
ISBN 978-1-76032-209-0

CONTENTS

TOP NOTES SERIES

This series has been created to assist HSC students of English in their understanding of set texts. Top Notes are easy to read, providing analysis of issues and discussion of important ideas contained in the texts.

Particular care has been taken to ensure that students are able to examine each text in the context of the module it has been allocated to.

Each text generally includes:

- Notes on the specific module
- Plot summary
- Character analysis
- Setting
- Thematic concerns
- Language studies
- Essay questions and a modelled response
- Other textual material
- Study practice questions
- Useful quotes

We have covered the areas we feel are important for students in their study of *Texts and Human Experiences* for their Common Module. I am sure you will find these Top Notes useful in your studies of English.

Bruce Pattinson
Series Editor

COMMON MODULE: TEXTS AND HUMAN EXPERIENCES

"It is quite possible—overwhelmingly probable, one might guess— that we will always learn more about human life and personality from novels than from scientific psychology"

NOAM CHOMSKY

What is the Common Module?

The Common Module set for the 2019–23 HSC is *Texts and Human Experiences*. It is compulsory to study this topic as prescribed by NESA and it is common to all three English courses. Remember: you will be learning how texts reveal individual and collective human experiences. There are no right or wrong answers in this module – it is about how you see and interpret material and engage with it.

In the Common Module you will be analysing one prescribed text and a range of short texts that are related to the idea of human experiences. You will analyse texts not only to investigate the ideas they present about this area but also how they convey these ideas. This means you will be looking closely at the techniques a composer uses to represent his / her messages and shape meaning. You will also be looking at relationships between texts in regard to the experiences you explore. Overall, you will become an expert on texts and the human experience—that is, the different notions people have about human experience and the various ways composers manipulate techniques to communicate their ideas about it.

Specifically you will look at one set text from the following list.

- Doerr, Anthony, *All the Light We Cannot See*
- Lohrey, Amanda, *Vertigo*
- Orwell, George, *Nineteen Eighty-Four*
- Parrett, Favel, *Past the Shallows*
- Dobson, Rosemary 'Young Girl at a Window', 'Over the Hill', 'Summer's End', 'The Conversation', 'Cock Crow', 'Amy Caroline', 'Canberra Morning'
- Slessor, Kenneth 'Wild Grapes', 'Gulliver', 'Out of Time', 'Vesper-Song of the Reverend Samuel Marsden', 'William Street', 'Beach Burial'
- Harrison, Jane, *Rainbow's End*
- Miller, Arthur, *The Crucible*
- Shakespeare, William, *The Merchant of Venice*
- Winton, Tim, *The Boy Behind the Curtain* Chapters: 'Havoc: A Life in Accidents', 'Betsy', 'Twice on Sundays', 'The Wait and the Flow', 'In the Shadow of the Hospital', 'The Demon Shark', 'Barefoot in the Temple of Art'
- Yousafzai, Malala & Lamb, Christina, *I am Malala*
- Daldry, Stephen, *Billy Elliot*
- O'Mahoney, Ivan, *Go Back to Where You Came From* – Series 1, Episodes 1, 2 and 3 and *The Response*
- Walker, Lucy, *Waste Land*

NESA has mandated that students must study a related text as part of the common module, and that this should be part of their in-school assessment. However there is NO LONGER a requirement to write about a related text in the HSC examination itself.

WHAT DOES NESA REQUIRE FOR THE COMMON MODULE?

The NESA documentation of the Common Module: Texts and Human Experiences states that students:

- deepen their understanding of how texts represent individual and collective human experiences;

- examine how texts represent human qualities and emotions associated with, or arising from, these experiences;

- appreciate, explore, interpret, analyse and evaluate the ways language is used to shape these representations in a range of texts in a variety of forms, modes and media;

- explore how texts may give insight into the anomalies, paradoxes and inconsistencies in human behaviour and motivations, inviting the responder to see the world differently, to challenge assumptions, ignite new ideas or reflect personally;

- may also consider the role of storytelling throughout time to express and reflect particular lives and cultures;

- by responding to a range of texts, further develop skills and confidence using various literary devices, language concepts, modes and media to formulate a considered response to texts;

- study one prescribed text and a range of short texts that provide rich opportunities to further explore representations of human experiences illuminated in texts;

- make increasingly informed judgements about how aspects of these texts, for example, context, purpose, structure, stylistic and grammatical features, and form shape meaning;

- select one related text and draw from personal experience to make connections between themselves, the world of the text and their wider world;

- by responding and composing throughout the module, further develop a repertoire of skills in comprehending, interpreting and analysing complex texts;

- examine how different modes and media use visual, verbal and/or digital language elements;

- communicate ideas using figurative language to express universal themes and evaluative language to make informed judgements about texts;

- further develop skills in using metalanguage, correct grammar and syntax to analyse language and express a personal perspective about a text

If this is what is required by NESA, we need to examine the concept of human experience carefully so we can adequately respond in these ways. I would recommend that you read the complete document which is on the NESA web site and can be downloaded in Word or Adobe. Understanding this document is an important step in handling the textual material within the guidelines required — remember you are reading for a purpose and should make notes and highlight ideas as you read so that you can develop these ideas later.

UNDERSTANDING THE COMMON MODULE

What are Human Experiences?

The concept of Human Experiences is at the heart of the Common Module.

Human Experiences are experiences of individuals or a group of people (eg a family, society, or nation) in life. There are a very wide range of human experiences which include but go beyond this list:

- feelings or reactions (momentary or long term): love, hate, anger, joy, fear, disgust
- key milestones or stages: birth, childhood, adulthood, marriage, divorce, death
- culture, belonging and identity
- conformity and rebellion
- innocence and guilt, justice
- freedom and repression
- education, vocation, work, sport, leisure
- attraction to a person, idea, group or cause
- opposition to an idea, cause, political system
- religious faith or belief
- extreme events such as an earthquake, avalanche, tsuanami
- regular events such as walking, eating, singing, dancing, discussing ideas.

The word *experience* seems innately connected to the human condition and it is something we have each day whether a mundane experience that is repetitive, or something new and dramatic which offers challenges and rewards. Experiences can vary greatly in their impact on individuals, groups and countries. One example might be a war that is a negative experience for a whole population while we may experience the wonder of medicine with a new vaccine for a deadly disease that saves millions of people. We need to note that the module asks for 'experiences' ...we are a combination of different experiences and each has a varying impact. One person's problem is another's challenge depending on perspective, skill set, previous experience and ability.

Experiences are widespread and often shared: this is why people tell their stories and these shared experiences form part of our cultural heritage. These experiences often inform, warn and teach across entire cultural groups and many stories are shared across cultures.

DEFINING HUMAN EXPERIENCES

Now let's attempt to define what human experiences are and shape them into a more coherent and easily understood framework so we can begin our investigation at a basic level of understanding before moving into more complex analysis and looking at how the texts illuminate our understanding of the term.

Dictionary.com defines the term **experience** as:

noun

1. a particular instance of personally encountering or undergoing something:

2. the process or fact of personally observing, encountering, or undergoing something:

3. the observing, encountering, or undergoing of things generally as they occur in the course of time:
    to learn from experience; the range of human experience.

4. knowledge or practical wisdom gained from what one has observed, encountered, or undergone, e.g. *a man of experience.*

5. *Philosophy*. the totality of the cognitions given by perception; all that is perceived, understood, and remembered.

verb

(used with object), **experienced, experiencing.**

6. to have experience of; meet with; undergo; feel, e.g. *to experience nausea.*

7. to learn by experience.

idiom

8. **experience religion**, to undergo a spiritual conversion by which one gains or regains faith in God.

Obviously there are a number of definitions according to context, but all are applicable to our study in some shape or form, as the range of human experience is so vast. The search for 'new experience' has driven much of the development of people, groups, cultures and nations over past millennia. New experiences are always met with excitement and often trepidation as to what change they might bring.

Think historically about how people have reacted to change. It can cause great upheavals in society, with violent reactions while other changes brought through various experiences are welcomed and may change how people live and comprehend the world. Experiences affect us emotionally in many cases rather than logically and when we respond emotionally, behaviours become unpredictable. This causes the paradoxes, anomalies and inconsistencies mentioned in the rubric. If we were logical beings the world would be an easier place, but probably more boring.

These definitions all point to the fact that memory is the key to experience. The experience is stored in memory and drawn upon when the circumstances are repeated or closely mimicked so we can deal with them — hopefully better than on the initial experience.

Experiences can come in many ways and the synonyms listed below for experience help us to understand the concept even further. They assist in defining how an experience can arise:

Synonyms

actions

understanding

judgment

background

wisdom

observation

contacts

acquaintances

perspicacity

involvement

actuality

practicality

know-how

caution

proofs

maturity

combat

savoir-faire

participation

doings

seasonings

patience

empiricism

sophistication

practice

evidence

strife

reality

existences

trials

sense

exposures

worldliness

skill

familiarity

forebearance

struggle

intimacy

training

inwardness

http://www.thesaurus.com/browse/experience?s=t

These synonyms show partly the vast array of words that our language has created around this concept, and also shows how important it is in the human psyche. We, as humans, want to experience. Now we will look at some examples of experiences and examine how they can have an impact. It is also important to remember that experiences do not have to be positive. You might experience a huge problem, a bereavement, a car accident, an unwelcome relationship or something totally bizarre that rocks your world. There can be a more opaque side to any experience that may need to be addressed.

The whole aim of this Common Module is to examine the text closely but also relate it to the concept of human experiences and decide how examining it in this way enables us to better understand both the text and the concept of humanity.

It is important that you unpack what each text you study shows you about human experiences and what ideas / themes arise from those experiences. Formulate your own ideas about the text.

Read the NESA Stage 6 document called *English Stage 6: Annotations of selected texts prescribed for the Higher School Certificate 2019–23* (see *www.educationstandards.nsw.edu.au*) for the set text you are studying. This document offers insights into the way each particular text should be examined by outlining key ideas and areas for clarification.

Human experiences and ways of experiencing vary due to individual circumstance and these experiences can change many things about individual lives, communities and the world. When we examine the concept of human experience in relation to a text, we need to examine the assumptions or biases we bring to it as well as how experiencing the text itself may change us and how we view things. The text may challenge and confront how we view the human experience or we may have preconceived ideas that make it more difficult for this to happen.

Students can also think about their own 'personal experience to make connections between themselves, the world of the text and their wider world.' Examining and enjoying any text is an experience in itself but it is what we take away from the text and apply that is the crucial aspect. That is not to say that every text will be enjoyed or offer a human experience that is significant either positively or negatively. Some texts may not personally engage you and that is fine. This is especially so when you begin to look for other related material that links to *Texts and Human Experiences*. We recommend that you find examples of texts that link but also personally appeal to you so that you can relate empathetically with them.

Individual Human Experiences

The idea of personal experiences is a popular and pervasive concept, especially in the literature of many cultures. Recording personal experiences as a means of sharing wisdom or more mundane daily tasks is part of human nature and we record and relate these experiences frequently. Experiences are recorded and relayed in many ways. We tell oral stories in both anecdotal and formal ways, we write, draw, sing and photograph our way into history (or not). Look at the proliferation of social media in this current century as people record their daily, even hourly, experiences for all to see. We record the most trivial details of our lives for likes and followers while the real world passes us by. Human experiences affect us on a daily basis and some experiences influence our lives and the way we live them.

Individuals seek out experiences in a variety of ways. Some seek more and more extreme experiences to test themselves against the world. Others limit their experiences. A lot of people prefer the familiar and don't actively seek new experiences. Individuals, it must be remembered, also see experiences in different ways and the same experience may have a very different impact on individuals. The one thing we can be certain about is that experiences are part of humanity and even the most limited of us have them. Many of these experiences also come from interaction with others and as noted we also like to share these experiences.

Experiences are what define us in many ways and are what makes us human.

We are going to look at four specific ways that experiences can influence us as people over the next few pages. These are physical, psychological, emotional and intellectual experiences and many experiences are a combination of these.

Physical Experience

The concept of a physical experience is tied into the human experience and part of the collective experience as well. Individuals seek physical experiences to test themselves against nature and other individuals often as part of trials and rituals, for example being integrated into a community. In modern times individuals have sought to test themselves with extreme sports and explorations into the harshest conditions and even space. Physical experiences can also change the way we see the world and others because of the chemical changes these experiences have on our bodies and mind. Physical experiences are often challenges and part of the experience is overcoming adversity. These physical challenges are often celebrated, as in the case of sports, but can also offer challenges if the experience is a negative one such as an accident or disease. Physical experiences are also often quite public and thus have permeated our societies in both their execution and how they are perceived. These physical experiences, even if experienced vicariously, have become popular across cultures and celebrated. Think of examples for yourself but most competitive sports offer examples.

Bruce Lee extends the concept of the physical experience into all aspects of life and that's what we will look at next in our analysis of human experiences –

'If you always put limits on everything you do, physical or anything else, it will spread into your work and into your life. There are no limits. There are only plateaus, and you must not stay there, you must go beyond them.'

Psychological Experience

The idea of a psychological experience is tied into many of the abstract ideas that people experience and can lead to a discussion of what is normal psychology. From the earliest times humans have attempted to alter their psychology through a number of experiences. On a simple level this can be a drug that changes the person's or group's perspective on reality. Examples of this might be alcohol or marijuana but cultural groups also use various substances to share group experiences. This can be seen in Native American cultures with *peyote*. In more modern times prescription drugs that are mood altering have been used to minimise the symptoms of psychiatric illnesses such as depression, and these mood altering drugs are common and legal. Others attempt to alter their psychology by seeing specialists in this area while others act out their condition leading to social and criminal issues. When discussing the human experience, psychology is a key issue and will form a part of most studies of experience. When taken too far this search for a new psychological experience can be harmful eg. an addiction.

Carl Jung, the famous psychologist, comments on the problems of addiction for human experiences, stating clearly that excess can be an issue:

"Every form of addiction is bad, no matter whether the narcotic be alcohol, morphine or idealism."

Emotional Experience

According to the psychologist, Robert Plutchik, there are eight basic emotions:

- **Fear** — feeling afraid.
- **Anger** — feeling angry. A stronger word for anger is rage.
- **Sadness** — feeling sad. Other words are sorrow, grief (a stronger feeling, for example when someone has died) or **depression** (feeling sad for a long time without any external cause). Some people think depression is a different emotion.
- **Joy** — feeling happy. Other words are happiness, gladness.
- **Disgust** — feeling something is wrong or nasty
- **Trust** — a positive emotion; admiration is stronger; **acceptance** is weaker
- **Anticipation** — in the sense of looking forward positively to something which is going to happen. **Expectation** is more neutral; **dread** is more negative.

https://simple.wikipedia.org/wiki/List_of_emotions

Emotions are the strongest drivers of human experience and form lasting aspects of any experience. Think about breaking up with someone you love and the emotions that drive behaviours in this situation. People have all sorts of extreme behaviours under the influence of emotions and these experiences are often the ones recorded and those which influence us most. Think about the role emotions play in our lives and the range of emotions from the list above. Consider how much emotions affect our life experiences, how they influence our decisions which decide our experiences and on a higher level consider how they affect the decisions which may seriously impact our experiences, such as politicians going to war.

Intellectual Experience

The concept of an intellectual experience is linked to decisions and experiences we have based on analysis and logic rather than the emotional choices referred to in the previous section. These intellectual experiences have changed the way we live and how we have seen our world. These experiences have affected the way we as humans have altered our world to suit our needs and lead to all the great advances in human society and thus experiences. Changes in our ideas, beliefs etc. alter the way we interact with the world and often these intellectual changes come at great cost.

Think of the time in Europe when the Church dominated and stopped scientific advances by calling them heresy/witchcraft. Open societies are more open to new ideas and this is what has hastened the pace of intellectual experiences as dominant ideologies fall away. Intellectual advances may not have the excitement that the other types produce but perhaps they have a more lasting impact on people, societies and the world in general. Ideas are powerful experiences and people hold beliefs strongly.

Immanuel Kant stated that:

"experience without theory is blind, but theory without experience is mere intellectual play."

Consider this statement in the light of what we have learnt about human experiences. Are they a combination of many factors or can we isolate experiences into simple forms?

What exactly is a human experience?

The titular question reminds us of the old brainteaser: "If a tree falls in a forest and no one is around to hear it, does it make a sound?"

There are two classic responses to this. The more Platonically-minded would say the tree always makes a sound when it falls in the forest. We don't have to be there to hear it; we can imagine the sound of a tree falling in the forest, based on memory of such an event or on the recording of such an event. We know that sound is just vibrating air, and it's safe to say that air always vibrates in response to a tree falling, or a bear growling, or a cicada singing, whether we are there to hear it or not.

The second answer is a more post-structuralist response: the sound doesn't occur on its own; it needs a human ear to be heard. Therefore, if there is no human in the forest to hear the tree fall, then there is no sound. This automatically implies that "experience" of anything requires the presence of a human being, which means there is no such thing as an experience that *isn't* human.

Animal rights activists – or anyone with a beloved pet – would almost certainly reject this notion because it prioritises humans and relegates all other species to a lower class of being: an attitude that most would agree has gotten the human race into an awful lot of environmental trouble over the last 200 years of industrialisation.

In his article (*What is an Experience?*), my learned colleague Paul Hartley describes experience in its most basic form, as "the perception of something else" and "ultimately information about what we have perceived." But does this make it particularly human? Dogs and cats perceive things. Insects perceive things. You could even say that plants perceive things, such as the direction from which the sun is shining. Perception is the most basic of life's survival tools for all manner of flora and fauna.

In her brief but cogent disquisition on the subject (*What is Human?*), another of my learned colleagues, Nadine Hare, asserts that to be human is a social construct. Hartley builds on that notion by suggesting that culture affects experience when we start to share it, because "the words, associations, and priorities we attach to the shared experience define how we understand the world we live in."

Hare rightly points out that this world is increasingly dominated by consumerism, which has distorted what it means to be human by excluding all of the attributes and qualities that "make people people." Calling us consumers reduces our experiences to mere transactions. It defines human experience within the narrow confines of the purchase funnel and has little interest in anything that isn't a purchase driver.

Perhaps the field of commerce is where the experiential rubber most emphatically meets the road. Unlike mere perception, commerce is a uniquely human experience. It has mediated, automated, and dominated the human agenda to the point where we are defined by what we buy and little else. Commerce has invaded the non-profit spheres of government, health, and education, imposing its own priorities and principles on these institutions in the expectation that they will behave more like businesses. And even though business still strives to appeal to the so-called masses, it prioritises the pursuit of individual wealth, and in so doing, not only inhibits the desire for shared experience but unravels the social fabric historically woven by the democratic tradition.

As if in response, that social fabric is being re-woven by our networks. As Hare asserts, "humans both produce technology and are produced through technology." Experience is shared more now than it ever has been because the experiential platform – i.e., that very human invention called the internet – is in place to facilitate it like never before, and on a global scale.

This sharing capability reintroduces all of those things that "make people people" back into the conversation – whether commercial or political. What "makes people people" is messy, unpredictable, emotional, and complex. Most of what makes us human has no place in the experiential confines of the purchase funnel, and defies any of our attempts to place it there.

The challenge for us as a species is to embrace this new capacity for sharing to keep the agendas of our hegemonic institutions – whether commercial or political – from defining what makes an experience human. A post-consumer business strategy might be one that, as Hare hopes, will "expand our view of people to include the complex and dynamic social, cultural, gendered, spiritual and racialised beings that they are." Maybe then will our shared human experience truly become, as Hartley asserts, the glue that holds us all together as human beings.

Will Novosedlik

MISC magazine

https://miscmagazine.com/what-is-a-human-experience/

This article appeared in the September 2014 edition of MISC magazine. Can you relate to what the article says about human experiences? Do human experiences depend on perception? Does the experience of anything require the presence of a human as experiencer (para 3)? Can the ideas of experience be extended to include perception by plants or animals? Hartley's idea is that "shared human experience" is "the glue that holds us all together as human beings". Is this an oversimplification?

The Impact of Human Experiences

Human experiences have impacts on many levels. On an individual level, we can have changes in our assumptions about the world and people around us; we can ingest new ideas and have these open new vistas of productivity and performance. We can also reflect and build on these experiences to ensure that they are even more meaningful to our lives. Behaviours towards others and the way we respond to the world can manifest themselves in new and different responses. An example might be that through adverse experiences we can build resilience so that the next negative experience isn't as traumatic and we accept it for what it is. Experiences also teach us new behaviours on a very physical level — if you burn yourself once on a flame you learn not to do it again (hopefully).

The impact of human experiences can also be shared in groups and societies. Firstly, let's examine some group dynamics that can be affected by human experiences. Groups share experiences and adapt and develop behaviours that impact on the group as a whole. Think about the notorious 'bonding' sessions sporting teams have that unite them in a common goal. Think about the behaviours of various gangs in our society. We see plenty of examples of this on American television where gangs based on ethnicity and social groupings form specific sets of behaviours that impact on how they interact with each other and the world. These groupings carry assumptions about how they see the world and respond to it. For example, they may have generally negative reactions to law enforcement and this is ingrained into their codes of behaviour. They are suspicious of the world and the people in it — dividing them up into threats, the law and victims. These behaviours are often reinforced by group experiences such as the initiation rituals which are integral to membership.

Often the impact of these behaviours is to perpetuate stereotypes that then categorise the individuals within these groups. The graphic I have included here shows a stereotypical gang member with the suspicious gaze, ubiquitous hoody and scruffy look. These stereotypes reject new ideas and maintain assumptions about the world, often to the detriment of their members. The experiences they have reinforce their own stereotypical way of viewing anything outside the safety of the group and the cycle continues. Of course, other groups have more positive impacts and see the world as a  very different place and their experiences are designed to be positive interactions. Think about groups such as Rotary who are constructive in the community. Other groups have specialty interests such as Animal Welfare, Surf Lifesaving and charities.

Normal social interactions impact groups and individuals, but it takes a major event to alter the behaviours of whole societies, especially so in the modern world where societies are large in scale. Earlier in human history smaller experiences could alter the behaviour of societies as they were insignificant in size compared to modern ones. We often fail to remember that many of these ancient societies' behaviours were impacted by superstition, religions and cultural habituation. The modern society as we know it is only a recent phenomenon. Just a few hundred years ago with church rule people were forced to think in a specific

way and punished for not adhering to a theological culture. Think of the Spanish Inquisition, the imprisonment of Galileo and other such restrictions on freedom of thought; scientific breakthroughs were hidden or declared witchcraft. Even recently the world has seen societies kept repressed by failed ideologies. The brutality of such regimes has left deep scars on the social psyche of nations as they try to recover. This has had an impact on the human experiences of whole populations, and societies respond accordingly.

One example might be at the conclusion of the Communist regime in East Germany when the Berlin Wall was destroyed as a visual symbol of the new-found freedom of a whole population of people who had been repressed for decades by a brutal and ever-present regime. Many citizens who had grown up in this system, where you could 'disappear' without trial or real evidence, found the idea that you could express yourself incredible. Many of the

East Germans couldn't believe that this freedom was real and that the Stasi (the secret police) were gone.

Other experiences can affect societies in extreme ways. Think about wars and the impact they have on civilian populations.

Climatic events such as earthquakes change the way that people behave and respond to situations. Catastrophic flooding occurred in the US city of New Orleans in 2005. The US President's response to help was not immediate and the national administration was severely criticised for lack of effective action.

Societies also respond to perceived problems such as pollution. In 1989 the oil tanker Exxon Valdez ran aground in Prince William Sound, Alaska with disastrous results. The effects of this event are still being experienced thirty years later.

Societies can be divided, as we saw with the election of Donald Trump in the United States of America and the reaction of the Political Left.

The impact of human experiences on societies can be quite dramatic, as we have seen, while other experiences (such as an election) can go by without a murmur from societies, no matter who wins. As a last thought before we move on you should also consider the impact of the media on societies in the modern world, and how they influence individuals, societies and the development of ideas.

Problems With Human Behaviour

So far, we have discussed the impact of human experiences on behaviour. Now we can begin to develop some more complex judgements and understandings about the impact of those experiences on human behaviours. In simplistic terms it could be assessed as:

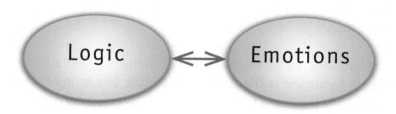

These two opposites on the continuum certainly shape the manner in which we see incidents and how they affect the experience. For instance, if someone you love has no interest in you, it creates a very different reaction to someone you don't care about having no interest in you. It is generally agreed that humans respond more strongly with emotion than they do with logic. Often, it is only through time and reflection that we can understand how an experience has changed and/or altered the manner in which we see a situation or individual.

The Role of Storytelling in Human Experiences

Storytelling has been part of the human experience since 'people' began communicating and it is a method used to convey information and experience as well as be entertaining. Earliest myths were all oral and then people began to write down stories so they weren't lost in time. From this, various theories have developed around storytelling and one is the 'monomyth', which is a template across cultures for storytelling. Let's have a look at this below.

'In narratology and comparative mythology, the monomyth, or the hero's journey, is the common template of a broad category of tales that involve a hero who goes on an adventure, and in a decisive crisis wins a victory, and then comes home changed or transformed.

The concept was introduced in *The Hero with a Thousand Faces* (1949) by Joseph Campbell, who described the basic narrative pattern as follows:

"A hero ventures forth from the world of common day into a region of supernatural wonder: fabulous forces are there encountered and a decisive victory is won: the hero comes back from this mysterious adventure with the power to bestow boons on his fellow man."

Campbell and other scholars, such as Erich Neumann, describe narratives of Gautama Buddha, Moses, and Christ in terms of the monomyth. Critics argue that the concept is too broad or general to be of much use in comparative mythology. Others say that the hero's journey is only a part of the monomyth; the other part is a sort of different form, or colour, of the hero's journey.

https://en.wikipedia.org/wiki/Hero%27s_journey

Storytelling in History and its Purpose in Human Experience

Storytelling in oral form was accompanied by some theatrics to make the stories as entertaining as possible. Many of the early narratives were based upon religious ceremonies and stories of the creation of the earth and people(s). As time moved on, these stories were accompanied by dance, music and/or theatre and often were part of lengthy rituals, often taking days. These stories were designed to bring meaning to people's lives by explaining their own existence and the purpose/meaning of life in a time when life expectancy was short and entertainment was scarce. Of course stories were also recorded as these experiences were significant to all people and these stories run across all cultures. Before writing, stories were recorded in pictures such as cave art, in tattoo designs on skin and in designs such as rock piles and the giant carved heads of Easter Island.

Writing changed the manner in which stories were told and many of the old oral traditions were lost, barely being kept alive by specialists. Stories began to travel across cultural and national boundaries on whatever surface could be created. Papyrus, bones, pottery, skins, paper and in more modern times film, video and digital storage have changed, over time, the way in which stories of human experience have been told and shared. Content evolved from myth, fable and legend to history, personal narratives and commentary. Modern narrative form often has an educational or didactic element and can drift into propaganda. Stories of self-revelation can be instructive and give audiences the opportunity to apply learning to individual lives, whereas historically narrative was used in this way for societies and groups as a whole. In recent times narratives have become interactive and audiences can choose how the narrative unfolds.

Whatever form the story takes we all have a seemingly innate need for narratives to make sense of our lives. They either confirm our world view or alter our world view depending on the experience they convey and the experiences that we bring to the narrative. We need to remember that narratives are important to human experience and have been significant since the beginning of time.

The Text as an Experience

The concept of the text as an experience is one area to consider as we look at *Texts and Human Experiences*. Reading or viewing the text is an experience in itself and when we do this we bring our own history (experiences) to the text and this helps shape our understanding.

Think about the personal perspective that you bring to a text. What are some of your experiences that might influence how you read a particular text? Some texts, especially personal narratives of trial and tribulation or loss, can be confronting to some audiences and bring back strong opinions or emotions. Many texts attempt to do this as they convey a particular point of view about the world.

Does what you bring to the text affect what you learn from that text? We also need to delve into how the narrative experience is conveyed and how this in turn impacts upon the manner in which the story is received by audiences across different cultures. For example, Western films where heroes fight Islamic terrorism may well be viewed very differently by audiences in Western democracies and Islamic countries. Even seemingly innocuous narratives like the movie 'The Red Pill' which is about men's rights and created by a woman, has caused a polarisation of views wherever it has been shown. Strong personal experiences and viewpoints certainly bring their own understandings to texts.

Questions for Texts and Human Experiences

- Define the module in your own words.
- How are people connected by shared experiences?
- How might physical experience(s) change the way you respond to the world?
- How do you think a person's context and prior experiences shape how they perceive the world?
- Are experiences unique or do prior experiences have an impact on a current experience and way of seeing life?
- What is positive about human experiences?
- Discuss what is negative about human experiences.
- To what extent does experience shape the way we see other people and / or groups?
- Is an individual's culture part of their experience or is it something else?
- Is it possible not to have any meaningful experiences at all?
- Why do people tell stories?
- What do you think you might learn from a narrative?

STUDYING A FICTION TEXT

The medium of any text is very important. If a text is a novel this must not be forgotten. Novels are *read*. This means you should refer to the "reader" but the "responder" can also be used when you are referring to the audience of the text.

The marker will want to know you are aware of the text as a novel and that you have considered its effect as a written text.

Remembering a fiction text is a written text also means when you are exploring *how* the composer represents his/her ideas you MUST discuss language techniques. This applies to any response you do using a novel, irrespective of the form the response is required to be in.

Language techniques are all the devices the author uses to represent his or her ideas. They are the elements of a fiction that are manipulated by authors to make any novel represent its ideas effectively! You might also see them referred to as stylistic devices or narrative techniques.

Every fiction uses language techniques differently. Some authors have their own favourite techniques that they are known for. Others use a variety to make their text achieve its purpose.

Some common language techniques are shown on the diagram that follows.

LANGUAGE TECHNIQUES

Setting – *where does the action take place? Why? Does the setting have symbolic meaning?*

Main Character portrayal/development: *How does the character develop?* **What is the reader to learn from this?**

Minor Character use: *How does the author use the minor characters to represent ideas about themes or major characters?*

Narrative Person: *what is the effect this has on the narrative and the reader's response to it?*

LANGUAGE TECHNIQUES

Humour

Symbols and motifs: *how is repetition of image/idea used to maximise the novel's effect?*

Images: *similes, metaphors, personification,*

Dialogue: *not just what is said but how it is important in representing ideas*

Tone: *not just of character comments but also of the narration*

Conflict: *the action, Man vs man, Man vs nature, and/or Man vs himself*

Aural techniques: *Alliteration, assonance, onomatopoeia and rhythm*

THE AUTHOR

George Orwell was the pen name of Eric Blair and he was born in India in 1903. As his father was part of the Civil Service his education followed the pattern of most of the English ruling India at the time and he was sent home to an English boarding school at the age of eight.

Orwell was a bright child and was allowed to attend a private school for the wealthy but later wrote that he had suffered from the social stigma of his parent's comparative poverty. He felt that the only reason he was allowed to attend the school was to gain honour for his school.

Orwell continued his secondary schooling at Eton where he was encouraged to explore many of the new ideas current in Europe at the time. In Europe post the First World War socialism and liberal philosophies were popular concepts with the intelligentsia. Orwell could have proceeded on to university but chose instead to join the civil service and was posted to Burma.

Orwell served as a sergeant in the Imperial Police Force but came to view the part he played, as being contrary to the manner authority should be wielded. He resigned and returned to England in 1927 after having served for five years in Burma.

George Orwell then chose to follow a path which he always found difficult to explain but he lived for a short while (a little over a year) with tramps in both England and France. This experience came to be the source of his first book, *Down and out in Paris and London*. Orwell married and for a time taught in an English school. He published two more novels *Burmese Days* and *Clergyman's Daughter* and though they were well received he was not yet self-supporting from his writing. He did, however, change jobs and became a clerk in a bookstore. It was at this time that he joined the Socialist Party.

When the Spanish civil war broke out between the fascists under General Franco supported by Germany's Nazi Party and the socialists, Orwell went to Spain as a reporter.

It was inevitable that he would join the Republican side (socialists). The Marxist affiliated group that he joined was anti-Stalinist in its orientation. The fact that there were different brands of socialist/communist groups led to much in-fighting and lack of trust between the anti-fascist groups.

The better known Communist International Brigade ultimately became Russian Communist controlled and under orders from Moscow set out to "purge' all the other socialist groups. The betrayals and executions embittered Orwell and many other socialists who had first-hand experience of the brand of

Communism which Stalin came to control and export from the U.S.S.R.

It was lucky for Orwell that he had been badly wounded in a battle with fascist forces because he avoided the period of assassinations by the communist groups on their socialist allies. Orwell and his wife nevertheless fled Spain fearing for their lives. The communists' betrayal of their fellows permanently coloured his perceptions of how a cause could be corrupted and betrayed for power and domination.

In 1939 he sold his first commercially successful book *Coming up for Air* that predicted the forthcoming Second World War. During the war Orwell continued to write even though much of his writing was as a journalist with his own regular column.

It was the publication of his satire *Animal Farm* that elevated him into the eye of the reading public. The novel was published in 1945 and has as much to do with the effects of socialist totalitarianism and its effects on the individual, as it has to do with the inner struggles and moral collapse of individuals.

The novel *1984* likewise deals with the totalitarianism of a future world. It was published in 1949, just one year before the author's death. The title of the novel is a reference to 1948, linking his life and times with a future time and reflecting his concerns for the future. For more information go to:

https://en.wikipedia.org/wiki/George_Orwell or

https://www.biography.com/people/george-orwell-9429833

SOCIALISM AND COMMUNISM

The difference between socialism and communism is an important distinction to make when looking at Orwell's novel and its impact on human experiences. Socialism has often been confused with Communism because at the outset the Communist regimes looked like they were socialist in belief.

So what then is Socialism? It refers mainly to the concept of ownership of both goods and property by the society in which the individuals live, rather than by the individuals themselves. This notion was first seen as early as in the fourth century B.C. and can be seen in the Greek philosopher Plato's work called *Republic*.

The same principles were also common in many tribal cultures where individual ownership was unknown and communal ownership was the accepted norm.

While socialism advocates the control of essential goods and services as well as the means of production it does not discourage ownership of goods and services. Socialist thinkers in England and Europe long advocated the social worth of a benevolent government system, which the intelligentsia at universities have long argued as one of the most moral systems of government. In contrast capitalism in its most severe form advocates a form of Darwinian survival of the fittest, without any form of social security and with the resources of a society owned by just a few people.

In its mildest forms many governments around the world have embraced some of socialism's philosophies.

We take for granted that there is a health care system and an education system and that there is some control over factories emitting pollution. These are all arguments for a socialist philosophy that has permeated our political structure and are now seen as norms.

It must be remembered that the world was a different place when Orwell was writing and although the industrial revolution had long since begun, society was dealing with the after-effects of rampant industrialisation and colonisation which culminated in the First World War.

The rise of the major totalitarian parties in Germany and Russia were, according to many historians, a direct result of the consequences of the First World War and the world wide economic depression caused by the Wall Street crash.

It is with this background we must turn to the birth of Communism and how it differs so radically from socialism in its effects. Communism as a distinct branch of socialism can be seen in the works of Karl Marx' *Communist Manifesto* (1847) and Friedreich Engel's *Das Kapital* (1894).

Very simply put, the major difference in ideas between Communism and Socialism stemmed from the notion that without *a power* struggle there would never be change. In the quest for power and control, as we see in the novel, the human experience is drastically and permanently altered by the state. Violent revolution was seen as the only viable means of overturning the ownership of the land, factories and minerals from the capitalists (the powerful, rich few). It is the change in the means of control of goods and labour which the communist revolution meant to bring to the world.

Socialism never encouraged violence as a means of social reformation and saw the means of change as a more subtle transition through education and good will.

SOCIALISM AND NATIONAL SOCIALISM

It must also be remembered that Hitler's political party, the Nazi Party, were also known, as the National Socialists but were violently opposed to Communism. This might provide an insight into how the philosophy of state ownership for the good of the people was at the heart of the German experience but that the concept of the Communist ideal was as far removed as could be.

Indeed in the Spanish Civil war in which Orwell fought, there were the German supported Fascists against the Communist and Socialist forces. (It is not often reported that the Communists betrayed their socialist allies in order to purge them.) These impacted on Orwell's vision of the world and thus the human experiences he writes about.

Orwell's Views

The problem was that in all the philosophical debate in Europe after the Soviet Revolution and the subsequent rise of Stalin to power in the U.S.S.R. (Union of Soviet Socialist Republics) many felt that this first government based on complete "socialist" principles should be given a chance even though many disagreed with all its theories.

The secrecy of the Stalin's Soviet regime meant that very few suspected the extent of the brutality towards the people in the years preceding the Second World War.

Indeed it is estimated that Stalin killed off more Russians and Soviet citizens than all of Hitler's invasion troops and the brutality of the Second World War managed to accomplish. Many who merely wanted a strong ally to a growing menace in Germany in the nineteen thirties were prepared to ignore the brutalities and shortcoming of the communist regime.

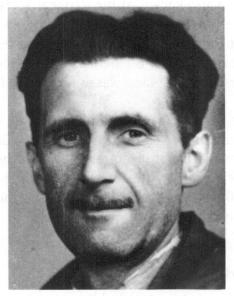

George Orwell

Orwell was not. Many of his earlier writings, before his critical acclaim, were devoted to an honest criticism as well as praise of the potential of socialist philosophies.

Many people only saw that Orwell supported some of the ideals of socialism and so thought of him as a dangerous left wing sympathiser, but in fact Orwell was very critical of the communist experience in Russia.

He saw that the system was flawed and that it had built a new ruling class, not on the lines of lineage as in the old feudal system but nevertheless equally as oppressive and totalitarian which would use any means in its power to "silence criticism" and "find scapegoats".

Orwell saw a post-industrialised society built on socialist principles as being able to improve the condition of the common man. However he also recognised that there was the potential for conflict, as the danger of a socialist society was in its principle of conformity. This would not recognise spiritual and psychological differences and hence the wellbeing of its individual members would suffer.

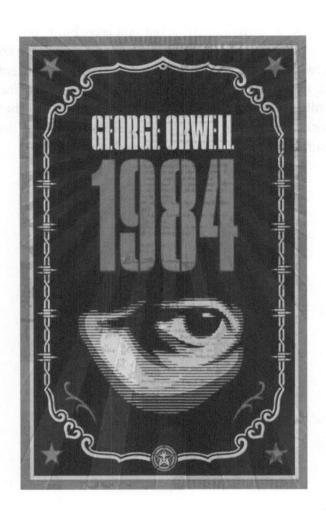

PLOT OUTLINE – CHAPTER SUMMARY

PART ONE

Chapter 1

- It is April 4th, 1984 and Winston Smith begins to write a diary, using an old fashioned notebook he found in an antique shop. In order to avoid being watched by the telescreen in his apartment, he sits in an alcove unseen by the screen, because although it is not illegal to keep a diary, "it was reasonably certain that it would be finished by death, or at least by twenty five years in a forced labour camp".

- He reflects on the Two Minutes Hate that occurred earlier in the week. It's a regular event in which workers at the Ministry of Truth are shown a video of the Enemy of the People, Emmanuel Goldstein, stimulating people into a regular frenzy of hatred.

- The girl with dark hair who works in the Fiction Department (and who Winston has never met but distrusts) sits behind him during the Two Minutes Hate. O'Brien, a member of the Inner Party, sits in the same row as Winston. During the two minutes O'Brien catches Winston's eye and the look suggests that O'Brien feels the same contempt for Big Brother and Winston feels sure he has an ally.

Chapter 2

- Mrs Parsons, the wife of Winston's neighbour, asks him to fix her kitchen sink. While at her apartment he notes that her son and daughter are typical products of the Youth League, and will probably denounce their mother to the Thought Police.
- The telescreen informs Winston of the good news of the defeat of a Eurasian army, followed by the news that the chocolate ration would be reduced from 30 grams to 20.
- Having started his diary Winston recognises that he is a dead man, but determines to stay alive as long as possible.

Chapter 3

- Winston dreams of his mother and baby sister. They are far below him, looking up at him as they sink further and further. He knows somehow that their lives were sacrificed for his own.
- His dream changes and he is now in the countryside. The girl with the dark hair walks towards him and flings her clothes aside. The movement captivates him as it suggests a discarding of Big Brother and the Thought Police.
- Winston wakes up and does the regular fitness exercises in front of the telescreen. As he does them he remembers one of his earliest memories, an air raid when he and his family hid in a Tube station underground. He realises that since that time war has been almost continuous, with Oceania swapping enemies occasionally between Eastasia and Eurasia.
- Any inconsistencies such as these are regularly rewritten by the Party, with nobody remembering the actual

events. Winston realises that the past no longer exists in any written form, or even in people's memories.

Chapter 4

- Winston begins his day's work at the Records Department at the Ministry of Truth, rewriting newspaper articles so that they don't contradict the Party's actions. For example the Ministry of Plenty promised there would be no reduction in the chocolate ration, so he substitutes the promise for a warning that there might be a ration reduction in April.
- One challenging task for Winston is to rewrite a speech of Big Brother's which refers to 'non-existent persons'. His task was to remove the reference to a comrade Withers who had earlier been eulogised in the speech for services to the state. The person Big Brother was referring to was probably vaporised, so Winston creates a glowing speech about a successful comrade (comrade Ogilvy) instead. Ogilvy had never existed but once Winston finishes his article he will have existed with as much certainty as Julius Caesar or Charlemagne.

Comment

The power to rewrite history is a common theme throughout the novel. Winston is obsessed with the past and with the authenticity of past events. Ironically, he is one of the people who perpetuate this deception by amending articles in "The Times" newspaper. By rewriting history the Party also has the ability to erase a person's existence or create an entirely fictional person (as in the case of Comrade Ogilvy). So the power to rewrite history is the power to create life and erase it, with no one being the wiser. Note in the opening how every aspect of human experience is noted by the state. Privacy is nigh impossible and the life experiences of people are controlled or manipulated for the benefit of the state. Winston's individuality marks him out in the reader's mind but we don't have high expectations for him because of the totality of control. Experiences outside the state controlled ones are crushed.

Chapter 5

- In the cafeteria at lunchtime, Winston talks to Syme who is from the Research Department. He is a philologist working on the Eleventh Edition of the Newspeak Dictionary. He's an expert on Newspeak and takes pride in the way hundreds of words can be eradicated and replaced with just one word.
- Syme explains that the aim of Newspeak is to narrow the range of thought and thereby make thought crime impossible, because there would be no words to express the thoughts.
- It dawns on Winston that Syme will be vaporised one day, because he is too intelligent and speaks too freely.
- Winston's neighbour, Parsons, joins them and asks for Winston's donation for Hate Week. He proudly tells Winston and Syme about his daughter who spied on a stranger while on a hike and turned him into the authorities.
- The telescreens in the cafeteria announce a message from the Ministry of Plenty: that the standard of living has increased by twenty percent. Winston wonders how anyone can believe this when only yesterday the chocolate ration was reduced. Winston wonders if

conditions have always been like this, or if people were better off years ago.
- The girl with the dark hair catches his eye in the cafeteria and Winston is afraid she is spying on him.

Comment

Newspeak provides the Party with the ability to narrow the range of thought as they narrow the English language. Power over someone's thought processes is the ultimate way to control their mind and thus their individuality. The Party uses Newspeak to strip a person of their ability to express their feelings and to eradicate dissent among the society. This chapter brings up the question of whether it is possible to think or feel emotions if there is no word to describe that thought or emotion.

The Party controls all information; therefore the 'facts' of the standard of living in Oceania cannot be refuted by anyone. Winston believes he can remember a time when conditions were better but nobody else seems to. This is because the Party controls information about the present and that past, and therefore shapes people's memories.

Chapter 6

- Winston writes another diary entry, about his encounter with an old prostitute three years ago. He reflects on the experience of having sex with his wife, Kathleen. Party members were discouraged from enjoying sex and are taught to tolerate it only for the sake of reproduction. The Junior Anti-Sex League encourages complete celibacy, with reproduction only through artificial insemination.

- The Party doesn't allow divorce, but encourages separation if there are no children being produced. Winston and his wife have been separated for almost eleven years.

Comment

The Party attempts to control even the most primitive instincts, like the sexual instinct. The power play at work here is between this natural human instinct and the state, which wants to curb all instincts that could prove more powerful than the Party. Desire, love, elation, jealousy and hatred are all strong emotions that can stem from a sexual relationship. All these emotions could prove more powerful than a duty to the Party, which is why sex is seen as a threat. When emotion is lost to the human experience life would seem hollow as Winston finds, it becomes automatic and unthinking which is what the Party wants.

Chapter 7

- Winston wonders whether the oppositional 'Brotherhood' really exists. He realises that if the proles had any idea of their own combined strength then they could overthrow the party easily. But the proles are not aware that they have anything to rebel against, because they follow the Party's propaganda. It is a Catch-22 situation: 'until they become conscious they will never rebel, and until after they have rebelled they cannot become conscious'.
- When reading a children's history textbook Winston wonders how much of it is true and how much is distorted by the Party's propaganda. The Party claims that people are now happier, more intelligent and have a better life than fifty years ago, but Winston knows the reality

doesn't match the supposed 'facts'. In his life there was only one occasion where he held absolute proof that the Party was lying. An article from 'The Times' contradicted the confessions of three revolutionary men, which meant that their confessions were fabricated, and their executions unjust.

- Winston understands *how* the Party changes history but not *why* they go to so much trouble to do so. In the face of changing 'facts', Winston knows that his freedom lies in believing what he knows to be true and remembering the past.
- Ultimate freedom is being able to say what you know to be true, or that two plus two equals four.

Comment

The proles far outnumber the Inner Party members and so could easily overpower the Party if they chose to. The Party has successfully disabled this power though, by allowing the proles a steady standard of living, complete with pornography, music, films, alcohol and the lottery.

Although they don't live in comfort, they are given just enough to ensure that they never contemplate rebellion. In this way the proles are never stirred into action and never aware of their own combined power.

Only once has Winston held evidence of a Party lie, but the fact that he did not use the proof for any purpose, shows that Winston realised he still had little power over the Party. His individual influence is not strong enough against the combined power of the Party.

The difference between individual influence and collective supremacy is a common theme in the novel. At this stage Winston believes that he has the power to control his own memories and therefore his own mind and that not even the Party can change this. This leads him to have some hope – a dangerous individualistic trait that could lead to experiences outside the permitted ones.

Chapter 8

- Winston decides to skip another Community Centre evening and goes walking through the proles' quarters in London. He enters a bar and buys an old man a drink in the hope of asking the man what it was like living years ago. But the man only remembers trivialities and nothing useful to Winston.
- He passes the junk-shop where he bought the notebook diary and buys a pretty, glass paperweight. He visits the owner's top room and sees that is would make a useful place to be alone and away from telescreens. Winston is intrigued by a poem that the owner, Mr Charrington, once knew; "Oranges and lemons say the bells of Saint Clement's...", but he can't remember the whole poem.
- When Winston leaves the shop and is walking home he passes the dark haired girl and becomes frightened because he's sure that she's following him. He contemplates killing her but decides against it.
- Winston believes that the Thought Police will come and get him that night.

Comment

The constant bombing of London streets provides a way for the Party to remind the proles of the war and that they need Big Brother to defend them. The bombs may be fired by the enemy or even by the Party, but either way the war provides a way for the Party to direct loyalty and devotion to Big Brother.

We also see in this final section the individualistic nature of Winston despite his seemingly innocuous characteristics. He thinks that he needs to do something with his life but is still afraid of the Party. Even his little gestures of defiance such as buying the paperweight are experiences that could see him punished. It is a world of tight controls, telescreens and ironically the Ministry of Love looms large over the city.

PART TWO

Chapter 1

■ Four days after visiting the junk shop, Winston passes the girl with dark hair in a corridor while at the Ministry. She falls down in front of him and while he helps her up she slips a note into his hand. Instead of being a note denouncing him as a thought criminal, it says, "I love you".

■ For the rest of the week Winston plans how to arrange a conversation with her. Eventually they manage to plan a day when they will meet out in the countryside.

Comment

The girl with dark hair exerts power of her own when she gives her message to Winston. She uses the Party's telescreens to provide a safe way to convey a traitorous message. This effectively reverses the power distribution by using the Party's own technology against them. Remember here that 'love' is banned and what they are doing is completely subversive – it is emotive and instinctual. Love is a common human experience and a strong motivating force.

Chapter 2

Winston and the girl meet in a secluded countryside clearing, after making their way there separately. He is at first incredulous that she should want to meet him like this and amazed to be kissing a woman who actually wants to be kissed and enjoys it. He finds out her name is Julia and that she does not keenly follow the Party's slogan but just puts on a very good act.

- Just as in his dream, Julia flings her clothes aside. He is glad to hear that she has slept with many men because it is contrary to the Party ideal and so gives him hope.
- Winston knows that it is this wild animal instinct that will bring down the Party, but because of this there is no such thing as pure love anymore because sexual acts are firstly political and secondly emotional.

Comment

By outlawing sexual relationships between Party members, the Party has made every sexual act have political significance and hence succeeded in dehumanising the act to an extent.

But similarly, the Party has also allowed Winston and Julia the power to express their rebellious emotions, which might have been denied had sex not been discouraged. It is also a powerful experience and has a strong impact on Winston, propelling him into further transgressions against the State.

At this point do you think there is any hope for Winston and Julia? Think about the Party's total control over all aspects of life and how any experience can be seen as subversive. Note also how it is changing Winston's thinking and he is beginning to question things around him more critically. The sexual relationship also makes him feel more confident. In light of what we know is this a false confidence?

Chapter 3

- Winston and Julia sometimes arrange meetings and try to hold intermittent conversations while walking down pavements. He finds out she is twenty-six years old, lives in a girls hostel and works in the Fiction Department which manufactures books and pornography. She doesn't have many memories of life before the Revolution and she hates the Party because it stops her from having a good time.
- Winston describes his wife but Julia already knows the type of woman because she was also taught to have the same attitude towards sex while in the Youth Movement. Julia thinks that the Party's attitude towards sex is so that people will never be relaxed or content but rather constantly on edge, and therefore susceptible to hysteria.

- Winston knows that the Party have similarly twisted the parental instinct and made the family dynamic one of distrust rather than love.
- Winston realises that it is only a matter of time before they are killed but Julia is more hopeful.

Comment

The theme of sexual power is continued with Julia's belief that the repression of the sex instinct allows the Party to channel that pent-up energy into hysterical behaviour. The Party has similarly subverted the role of the family, so that family members do not remain loyal to one another, but rather spy on each other.

The Party harnesses more power by channelling this devotion one normally feels for a family member to the patriarchal figure of Big Brother instead. From this we can gather that humans need experiences to be satisfied with life and this is why the Party attempts to control those experiences by manipulating and minimising them.

Chapter 4

- Julia and Winston meet at the little room above Mr Charrington's shop for the first time. Julia brings real sugar, coffee, tea, bread and jam that she bought on the black market. She also has makeup and perfume that she puts on herself.
- Julia completes a little more of the nursery rhyme that Mr Charrington began because her grandfather used to sing it.

Comment

Winston and Julia exercise their individual powers of thought when they devise a plan to meet at Mr Charrington's shop. It is the first time they have used this location and their meeting goes smoothly, without raising any suspicion. The positions of power seem to shift a little when it appears that they might have out-smarted Big Brother.

Do you feel that the experiences they have in the bedroom holds any future? Is Julia right to think that they can have these experiences without any consequences? Do you see their tryst as innocent experience? How might the State see it?

Chapter 5

- ■ Syme no longer comes to work and has presumably been vaporised.
- ■ Everyone is very busy with preparations for Hate Week. Pamphlets are being written, banners created and war songs composed. There are huge new posters of a Eurasian soldier (with Mongolian features) hung from buildings all over the city.
- ■ Since meeting Julia, Winston has stopped drinking so much gin, has put on weight, his varicose ulcer no longer itches and he no longer has coughing fits. He and Julia feel like they have their own little hiding place above Mr Charrington's shop, but they know that it cannot last long. The experiences he is having with Julia are changing him positively but the taint of despair that runs through the whole society is clear in the manner they interact.

- Julia believes that everyone secretly hates the Party and so she thinks Winston should approach O'Brien and offer his services. But she believes that Goldstein and the underground army doesn't exist but was invented by the Party as a scapegoat.
- In some ways she is less susceptible to propaganda and even thinks that the war is probably not happening, an idea that has never occurred to Winston. At the same time she doesn't think it is very important that the Party changes history, because she knows that the Party talks nonsense and the past isn't relevant to her.
- Winston realises that the Party's doctrine is easier to swallow for people who are uninterested in their surroundings.

Comment

There is a change in the power dynamic between the Party and Winston, shown by his improvement in health. His relationship with Julia has improved his quality of life and made his life more worth living, dragging it from the tedium and drudgery that we saw at the beginning of the novel. These experiences have made him whole in a sense and show the power of positive experiences on the human psyche.

The Party aims to maintain people's lives at a strategically wretched level so Winston's health improvements are an indirect blow to the Party. He and Julia's relationship give them both something more to live for, but ironically also brings them closer to death, with the threat of capture always imminent.

Chapter 6

- While at work, O'Brien invites Winston to his house to look at the new edition of the Newspeak Dictionary. O'Brien writes down his address on a piece of paper and this is all conducted in front a telescreen. Although Winston is glad to finally have this invitation, he knows that he is moving closer towards his grave.

Comment

Winston has wondered about the Brotherhood and this invitation of O'Brien's might answer all his questions, but at the same time it might be a trap to implicate himself as a rebel. O'Brien is an important Inner-Party member and has the power to arrest Winston, so Winston must trust his powers of intuition when it comes to trusting O'Brien. Do you think Winston's life experiences make him capable of judging this?

Chapter 7

- Winston wakes up crying next to Julia. He had been dreaming of a Jewish woman trying to defend her son being shot. It was a scene from a film he had watched and reminded him of his own mother. The way his mother put her arm around his weak baby sister was futile but still meaningful.
- The Party has persuaded everyone that primitive emotions, such as loving and nurturing, are pointless. Only the proles still feel these primitive emotions such as loyalty to one another and this makes them more human. Emotions stem from experiences and these are where the threat to the established order comes from.

- He and Julia decide that although they may be caught and forced to denounce each other, the party is unable to enter their heads and change their beliefs and feelings. Their feelings are unchanging and these primitive feelings make Winston and Julia human.

Comment

The Party has the power to inhibit people's natural emotions, by changing the nature of a family and people's friendships with others, but can they eradicate these feelings?

They haven't succeeded in removing Winston and Julia's feelings, so who is to say that others are also not hiding their true natures? This is something the Party is afraid of, so they try to read people's faces, because they cannot read their minds.

Winston and Julia believe that they have control over their own minds, and that the Party cannot change their emotions. People's independent minds are seen as a serious threat, which is why so much effort is spent of Party propaganda in order to influence those minds.

As long as rebellious minds pose a threat to the Party, they also contain power. Having power over one's own thoughts and actions is the ultimate threat to the Party, which wants to have complete control over every human function and capability.

Chapter 8

- Winston and Julia finally visit O'Brien in his home and are amazed at the opulence of an Inner Party member's house. They both drink wine for the first time when

they toast to Emmanuel Goldstein, the leader of the Brotherhood. Before this, neither of them had known for sure whether Goldstein was a real person or not.
- Winston and Julia agree to do anything the Brotherhood asks of them, except separate from each other.
- O'Brien explains that they will never know the reasons for their orders, because the less they know, the less they can confess when they are caught. They will never see the results of their actions because it is a slow process that will only be fully realised in many years' time.
- O'Brien arranges for a man to hand Winston a briefcase with the copy of *the book* that Goldstein wrote, which outlines the nature of the Brotherhood and their broad strategy for overcoming Big Brother.
- As a final question, Winston asks O'Brien if he knows the poem that starts "Oranges and lemons say the bells of St Clement's" and O'Brien completes the rest of the poem.

Comment

When visiting O'Brien's home, it becomes evident what luxury and power an Inner Party member possesses. Winston and Julia are both amazed that O'Brien can turn off the telescreen whenever he chooses. The fact that O'Brien's powerful position is being used to undermine the Party provides a sense of hope.

Chapter 9

- On the sixth day of Hate Week, when the city was in its biggest frenzy of hate, it was announced that Oceania was not at war with Eurasia, but Eastasia. The crowd assumes that the posters around the city of a Eurasian soldier were the sabotage work of Goldstein.

- With this change, the people in the Records Department have to work eighteen-hour days to change the political literature from the last five years which are now obsolete. After six days of solid work the job is finished and Winston is able to take the book to Mr Charrington's room.
- The book explains the boundaries of the three super-states of Eurasia, Eastasia and Oceania. They have been at war for twenty-five years and the nature of the war is primarily over the issue of boundaries of certain lands. The resources and cheap labour of these lands make them desirable targets to conquer and the super-states are constantly fighting over them.
- The war will never cease because there is no actual reason for the war, hence no reason for it to stop. The three super-states are roughly equal in wealth and any gains that a defeat brings only goes to producing more weapons with which to fight again.
- The aim of constant warfare, as directed by the Inner Party, is to maintain a hierarchical society. When machines were invented, they sped up the output of goods and this resulted in an increase of the quality of life among the lower classes.
- More leisure time and wealth would result in the lower classes becoming literate and realising that they have no need for the upper class minority. So constant warfare keeps the masses working hard to produce goods that will never be consumed by the population, nor will it result in any improvement to their living conditions.
- Science has not progressed but has even regressed because scientific discovery requires an inquisitive, intelligent mind and this conflicts with the principles of IngSoc. The party has two aims: to conquer all the lands

on the earth and to eliminate the use of independent thought among the masses. Therefore scientific thought only exists in the fields of weapon technology and psychological probing.

- The impossible aim of all three super-states is to strike a pact with one ally and then defeat them with a surprise attack of atomic bombs. Then they would make a pact with the last state and bomb them similarly, until the one state rules the world.
- The frontiers never really extend far beyond the enemy line because if they conquered another land then the two cultures would mix and each would realise that the other culture is the same and not the cruel barbarians the Party portrays them as being. It is integral to paint the enemy as being fundamentally different and sinister in order to maintain a war.
- Continuous warfare is used to keep the society exactly as it is, with no improvements and little threat from the other states since all states remain roughly equal in strength. The static nature of this society is reflected in the Party slogan: *War is Peace*.
- The difference between IngSoc and totalitarian regimes in the past is that with the invention of two-way transmitting televisions it is now possible to keep society under total surveillance.
- The social pyramid of Oceania:
    - Big Brother, who acts as a focal point for love, admiration and devotion
    - Inner Party, who are the brains of the state
    - Outer Party, who are the hands of the state
    - The Proles, who are the lowest class and mostly uneducated.

These social groups are not fixed by heredity. Oceania is under an oligarchic rule, which means being ruled by a group of people. Party members are not chosen by birth, but by fitting the ideology of IngSoc.

- The reason for changing history is so that no one can compare present society to the past. No one can then realise that the Party is lying about the supposed improvements in living conditions.
- If the Party were to be seen to change their minds, it would be a sign of weakness, so changing the past maintains the illusion that the Party's doctrine is consistent.
- The Newspeak words *crimestop, blackwhite* and *doublethink* are methods used by the mind to remain faithful to IngSoc ideology in the face of conflicting Party propaganda. The higher up the social ladder, the more competent are people at believing in contradictions. For example Inner Party members, support the war the most passionately, even though they know better than anyone else that the war is futile.
- Julia had come in while he was reading and had now fallen asleep, so Winston stops reading aloud. He gets up and looks out the window to the lady singing in the yard. Winston thinks again that the future lies in the proles.
- Julia has now woken up and stands next to him. Suddenly a voice begins speaking and they discover that there is a telescreen behind the picture on the wall. The house is surrounded and members of the Thought Police, led by Mr Charrington, capture them.

Comment

The Party's ability to shift a whole crowd's perception is evident when they break the news that Oceania is now at war with Eastasia. Individual experiences can be manipulated en-masse by propaganda.

The Party's quest to establish a long lasting hierarchical society is so that the highest members will always hold power over those beneath them. They are motivated by the idea of complete power over all the lands on the earth and power over people's minds. That was their power would be complete and unbreakable. The condition the world is in is a result of an unrelenting quest for authority and control. In order to obtain such power it became necessary to use the art of doublethink.

The key to the Party's power is for its Inner Party members to really believe the conflicting things they say, that way they are totally committed to what they do and are not distracted by logic. For example the Party is united in its attempt to conquer all enemies, despite the fact that this is logically impossible. As in the case of real-life cults, illogical and fanatical behaviour can take hold over people, irrespective of logical thought.

So now we know the basics of the state and how the Party is structured to eliminate competition and any threat to the status quo. Ignorance limits people's initiative and eliminates any individual thought processes. It is interesting to note that, like the socialism and communism that we discussed earlier, Winston sees the proles (proletariat) as the hope for change.

How do you see this hope at this point in the novel? How do the proles appear to you? Is Winston's hope based on his relationship and newfound freedoms?

Think about the conclusion to this part of the novel and its abrupt ending when the flat is raided. Why might Orwell have shaped the narrative in this manner? Where you surprised by this twist in the narrative or was it inevitable in your view?

PART THREE

Chapter 1

- Winston is imprisoned in a crowded cell at the Ministry of Love. He doesn't know how long he has been there, but he has seen many people arrive and then be taken to the dreaded Room 101. These include his old colleague Ampleforth and his neighbour Parsons, whom Winston thought would never be arrested.
- Winston holds onto the thought that O'Brien will save him somehow and perhaps send him a razor blade. The constant artificial light makes Winston realise that this is the place with no darkness where he dreamed he was to meet O'Brien.
- This becomes true, but not in the way Winston expected. Winston has been deceived and O'Brien leads the guards into the cell to beat Winston.

Comment

The novel is at its most hopeful while Winston reads the book but our hope is suddenly stripped away when he and Julia are arrested. When Winston is in the cell at the Ministry of Love it becomes painfully clear that there is little hope left for him, save for O'Brien sending him a razor blade. Then even that hope is crushed when O'Brien walks in and it becomes clear that he was never part of the Brotherhood.

It was all an elaborate scheme to give Winston the feeling he had the power to evade the Thought Police, which gave him hope before stripping it all away again. Having hope taken away is probably worse than never having hope at all. Hope is a human experience that is positive and now that is gone Winston has nothing to sustain him through his imprisonment.

Chapter 2

- Winston's torture begins and continues for an unknown number of days. Winston confesses to anything they accuse him of, such as espionage, murder, embezzlement and perversion.
- O'Brien tells him that he has been watching Winston for seven years and that the time has now come to make Winston perfect. With the aid of electrical shocks, O'Brien begins to train Winston in the art of doublethink tries to cure his 'defective memory'. He quizzes Winston on the war with Eastasia and the existence of the past.
- Winston believes that the past exists in human memories but O'Brien tells him that the Party controls all memories and therefore controls the past. O'Brien tries to control Winston's mind by forcing him to see that two plus two

fingers equals five fingers. Each time Winston answers 'four' he receives an increasing volt of electricity, until eventually he honestly cannot tell the number of fingers O'Brien is showing.

■ Even after this torture, Winston feels a deep relationship with O'Brien, as if he can really talk to him and be understood. O'Brien tells Winston that the point of all this is not punishment or to seek confessions, but to cure people and make them sane.

■ No one is allowed to die without first becoming wholeheartedly devoted to Big Brother. In this way, the rebel is no longer able to die with his convictions and become a martyr.

Comment

The Party has the power to enforce consensus reality, i.e. when something is defined as being real if it is what the majority believes to be real. They have the power to label Winston as insane, because he does not believe in the consensus reality that the Party imposes. O'Brien believes this is a valid diagnosis because "Whatever the Party holds to be the truth is truth".

The Party exercises a control that is both frightening and all-encompassing, that is the power over what is considered to be reality. Winston has nothing and they can make him think anything they want as he has nothing even his own thoughts as we see in the following example;

Winston once wrote "Freedom is the freedom to say that two plus two make four", so the blurring of this ability when under O'Brien's torture is a signal that what little power Winston used to have over his mind is being taken away.

Chapter 3

- "There are three stages in your integration', said O'Brien. 'There is learning, there is understanding, and there is acceptance. It is time for you to enter upon the second stage". Winston has learned that Oceania has always been at war with Eastasia and that two plus two equals five, but now it is time to understand *why* the party acts as it does.
- The Party does not seek power for the good of the majority or for wealth and happiness. Power is sought for its own sake, so that there will always be ways to exert suffering on others, which asserts the Party's dominance.
- Their power is collective in that it is held by the Party and not by any individuals. The axiom, "Freedom is Slavery" means that being alone, or free, is being powerless. But being at one with the Party means you are invincible and immortal, because the Party will always exist. If you are against the Party, not only will you die but you will never have existed according to history.
- Winston still does not believe this and thinks that the spirit of Man will save the human race from an eternity of oppression. O'Brien's argument to this is to show Winston how weak his body has become since being imprisoned, and that his mind is similarly weakened. But Winston maintains that he still has not betrayed Julia.

Comment

All the themes of individual control (power, coercion, propaganda, surveillance, spying and manipulation) come to a head in this chapter, as Winston is finally taught why the Party seeks so much control. The Party seeks power entirely just to have power, which is it is not the means to an end, it is the end itself. The hierarchical society allows them to exert their authority on the lower classes and thus makes them feel superior.

O'Brien says that only when people are suffering can you be sure that they are obeying your will and not their own, because to suffer would never be anyone's natural instinct.

Winston believes that human nature has the power to defeat the Party, but O'Brien says that the Party creates human nature. If this were true, then the people of Oceania would have no power of their own and be doomed to be oppressed forever. Winston realises that to die hating the Party is his last chance for power.

Winston has confessed and told them everything about Julia but he has not stopped loving her and it is these human feelings that are most deplorable to the Party. Holding onto thee feelings makes him more human and represents a part of his mind that has not been brainwashed.

As long as Winston has any small amount of power over his emotions, he will remain alive. They will only shoot him when he is completely changed. Emotions stem from remembering his time and experiences with Julia and this needs to be eliminated to make the Party supreme.

Chapter 4

■ Winston's period of torture has ended and he is left in a cell for several months. He is fed well and begins to regain his strength. He does physical exercises as well as mental ones, such as writing 'Freedom is Slavery', 'Two plus two equals five', and 'God is Power'. His mind has not fully succumbed to the brainwashing because one night he wakes up, screaming Julia's name. After that O'Brien enters Winston's cell and takes him to Room 101.

Comment

It appears that Winston's feelings for Julia mean that he still has a degree of power over his own mind, because otherwise O'Brien would not bother with him anymore. But O'Brien takes him to Room 101 to finish the brainwashing process and eradicate these last emotions.

Chapter 5

- Winston learns that Room 101 means something different for each person who goes there to be tortured. It always contains the person's worst fear, and in Winston's case that fear is of rats. Just as the cage of rats is being fitted onto his head Winston yells "Do it to Julia! I don't care what you do to her. Tear her face off, strip her to the bone. Not me!" O'Brien removes the cage and he has won because Winston betrayed the last feelings that were making him human.

Comment

Winston has now suffered the final degradation. He has undone his feelings for Julia and has now got nothing to live for or any power over his own mind because they have eradicated his emotions.

Chapter 6

- Winston sits at the Chestnut Tree Café, drinking Victory Gin and waiting for news from the telescreen about the war in Eastasia. He remembers seeing Julia once after he was released from the Ministry of Truth. They no longer have any emotions at all, let alone feelings for each other, and talked briefly about the fact that they both betrayed each other.
- Winston has been given a better job but does not have the motivation to attend his work very often. His life is meaningless and he spends most of his time in the Chestnut Tree Café, playing chess, drinking gin and listening to the news. Another victory is announced on the news and Winston feels elated. The novel ends with Winston looking up at the face of Big Brother; "The struggle was finished. He had won the victory over himself. He loved Big Brother".

Comment

Now that Winston has no power over his mind, he is no longer a threat and is released. Everything is dead inside Winston, just as O'Brien promised in the previous chapter. He is hollow and is waiting until the moment when he is filled up again by the Party. Winston has no interest in anything except the progress of the war, and the victory announcement channels his feelings into a complete and utter devotion to Big Brother. By loving Big Brother, Winston "has won the victory over himself" but really it is the Party who has won the victory over Winston. They have used him to exercise their own power because as O'Brien said in Part 3, Chapter 2, "power is in tearing human minds to pieces and putting them together again in new shapes of your own choosing".

The Party have filled Winston's mind with love for Big Brother, the transformation is complete, and they now have complete own him, physically, intellectually and emotionally and he can have no experiences without their control.

CHARACTER ANALYSIS

- Winston Smith
- O'Brien
- Julia
- Mr Charrington
- Big Brother
- Emmanuel Goldstein
- Mr Parsons
- Syme
- Ampleforth

Winston Smith

Winston is the protagonist and narrator. He is thirty-nine years old and works in the Records Department at the Ministry of Truth. As a member of the Outer Party he is not privy to the reason *why* the Party acts as it does, nor does he have the luxury of ignorance, as do the proles. He feels as if he is the only one who remembers that life used to be better in the past by the does not know how to use this information against the Party.

He has faith that human nature can defeat the Party, but it is this faith that leads to his capture, as it is O'Brien and Mr Charrington who denounce him. Winston's faith in human nature makes him more genuinely human than the others and his heroic character provides hope in the novel. His experiences outside the order of the state are the driving force in the novel and the means by which Orwell conveys his ideas about abuse of power and the problems individuals face when they experience this power.

O'Brien

O'Brien is a member of the Inner Party, whose sympathetic manner fools Winston into believing that O'Brien is a member of The Brotherhood. Unfortunately Winston discovers that O'Brien has been watching him for seven years and has orchestrated his capture by the Thought Police.

Although Winston is tortured by O'Brien, he still feels a devotion to him as the only person who really understands him. Winston describes O'Brien as a father, teacher and confessor, and this attitude is an important component of Winston's brainwashing program. Winston's devotion to O'Brien is then channelled towards a devotion to Big Brother.

Julia

Julia is an attractive twenty-six year old woman who appears to be a devoted follower of Big Brother. She contributes to community events and works hard at her job in the Fiction Department. Julia perpetuates this show of devotion to the Party so that she can indulge in unlawful activities without suspicion.

She enjoys sex and her relationship with Winston begins as a political act against the state but they end up forming a deeper bond. Both say that they will always stay true to their feelings, but once captured they both succumb to torture and betray each other. The experiences they have seem to form a bond between them but in the pressure of imprisonment and torture they give each other up. Some experiences are more powerful than others.

Mr Charrington

Mr Charrington owns the second-hand shop where Winston first found the notebook he uses as a diary. His shop is in a prole neighbourhood and Winston and Julia use the room above his shop as a safe meeting place. Mr Charrington, however, is a member of the Thought Police and the two are arrested in the room over his shop.

Big Brother

He is the figurehead of the Party and the object of people's affections in Oceania. His face is on huge posters all over the city of London, as well as on stamps, coins, cigarette packets, books and telescreens.

He has black hair and a black moustache and his eyes seem to follow you. Winston questions O'Brien as to whether Big Brother is a real person and his answer suggests that he exists only if one uses *doublethink*.

Emmanuel Goldstein

Goldstein is the supposed leader of The Brotherhood and the enemy of Big Brother. He was one of the original leaders of the revolution but was denounced as a traitor and fled into exile. It is unclear as to whether Goldstein still really exists, or whether his figure is used by the Party as a convenient scapegoat although it is more likely the latter. There seems to be no evidence but he is a convenient figure to create experiences for that can be used as propaganda.

Mr Parsons

Parsons and his family are Winston's neighbours and he also works with Winston in the Ministry of Truth. Parsons is plump, perpetually enthusiastic and rather stupid. He is, however, very loyal to Big Brother and Winston believed Parsons would never be arrested because he is "one of those completely unquestioning, devoted drudges on whom, more even than on the Thought Police, the stability of the Party depended".

Winston is very surprised then to see Parsons led to the cell in the Ministry of Love. He was denounced by his daughter but is proud of her for doing it, and grateful to be arrested. He is an excellent example of an unthinking plebeian who has no original thoughts or experiences and doesn't want them. He is happy to sacrifice his existence for the state and is exactly the kind of individual that the state wants and tries to create. In every way he is a success story of this new world order.

Syme

Syme is a philologist working in the Research Department on the Eleventh Edition of the Newspeak Dictionary. He is very clever and enjoys eradicating hundreds of words from the English language and replacing them with just one word. He disappears one day and Winston thinks that he was probably vaporised because he was too intelligent and spoke too freely. Intelligence is not required in a one party state just blind obedience. Intelligence is a threat and needs to be eliminated, which is what happens to Syme.

Ampleforth

Ampleforth is a poet who works with Winston in the Ministry of Truth. Winston meets him in the cell at the Ministry of Love. He was arrested because he allowed the word 'God' to remain at the end of a line from one of Kipling's poems, because he could not find another word that would rhyme. Even something as simple as this is a threat to the state – we can't imagine reading the word 'God' as a subversive experience – but the state as it is in the novel can't take any risks as we see with their thorough destruction of Winston's humanity.

THEMATIC CONCERNS

Human Experiences

Human experiences in *Nineteen Eighty-Four* show us that Orwell believed in individual experience and thought that the excessive, controlling totalitarian regimes that tried to manipulate human experiences were having a negative impact on the world. The novel is set in a particular context but it is still very much relevant to today, perhaps even more so with the increase in the ability and willingness of governments to watch their citizens. While Orwell's constant surveillance was impossible in his day now it is imminently possible and very probable. We have learnt this through Snowden's exposé of the NSA and organisations such as Wikileaks.

The word 'Orwellian' has become part of human lexicon with its meaning entrenched in the way we think. It can be defined as,

> **"Orwellian"** is an adjective describing a situation, idea, or societal condition that George Orwell identified as being destructive to the welfare of a free and open society. It denotes an attitude and a brutal policy of draconian control by propaganda, surveillance, misinformation, denial of truth, and manipulation of the past, including the *"unperson"*—a person whose past existence is expunged from the public record and memory, practised by modern repressive governments.
>
> https://en.wikipedia.org/wiki/Orwellian

So if we understand this is how the Party in the novel tries to control human experiences we can begin to think about how Winston and Julia subvert the state until they are captured, imprisoned and tortured for daring to step outside the norms of what was socially acceptable in such a society. All human experiences are under the control of the Party and this is to manage the people for the sake of power as O'Brien explains clearly to Winston in the text.

Any experiences which contain emotion (such as love) are regarded as subversive and need to be eliminated. Emotions need to be controlled and thus the 'hate' sessions which are used to divert any positive emotions or thoughts about society. We see intelligence and independent thought are negatives and can lead to being 'vaporised' both physically and historically. Experiences are things that you are told to have and even that may change with the current needs of the government and the state of propaganda.

We can see fleeting glimpses of positive human experiences in *Nineteen Eighty-Four* but we feel there is always an underlying sense of despair and the feeling that it won't end well. If Winston and Julia are in 'love' and some critics argue they can't know what that is, we still think that there is no hope in the relationship in such a society. Even Winston's change through the experience which is very positive cannot alter the whole structure of society and his misplaced hope in the proles doesn't give the reader a sense of change.

Examples of negative experiences abound in the novel and not just the horrors of Room 101. The whole society is held down, depressed and repressed. Now let's move on and see how a few other ideas impact on the human experiences in *Nineteen Eighty-Four*.

Manipulation and Human Experiences

Orwell stresses the visual drabness of life in the first chapter and we can see that the Party uses its ability to take control of the psychological experiences of the people in many ways. The first is the names of the buildings which e.g. Victory Mansions which are certainly not mansions but little one or two roomed apartments.

This accommodation, which smells of boiled cabbage and old rag mats is for privileged persons who belong to the Party. The contrast between the drabness of their lives and the squalor of the proles is an element of social control, which provides a means of maintaining power and privilege in the hands of the few.

The psychological domination of the Party by its various ministries is the central thrust of the novel and provides an easily recognisable means of control for society over the individual. The enigmatic figure of Big Brother who is at once reminiscent of the moustachioed Stalin and the charismatic hypnotic-eyed Hitler is an easily recognisable figurehead for a totalitarian party structure.

There is more to the personae of Big Brother than just a figurehead because it is evident that he may not even exist other than as a focus for the devotion of the people. Big Brother is a figurehead whose creation enables the focus of the adoration and loyalty of the society where there is little else to love.

The phrase or slogan "Big Brother is watching you" is at once a comfort and a threat. The stern father figure who watches over his people is implied but it is also understood that any deviation from Big Brother's rules is going to be observed.

As for the rules of this society we see a manipulation of the institutions of society where the individual is kept in a state of confusion. There are no fixed laws which are codified or written down so that at any time the Party needs to change a policy it can do so at will. The sense that laws are not fixed but operate at the whim of the Party is indeed a means of ensuring that power is never devolved from the institution of the Party. In a sense it is a society where the ultimate "rights" of the individual have been acceded to the "common good" which in this case is the Party machine. This shows us how individual experiences are crushed and group experiences are also controlled.

War as Part of Human Experiences

The three super powers Eurasia ruled by the Neo-Bolshevik Party, Eastasia ruled by the Death-Worship Party and Oceania by the Ingsoc standing for English Socialism Party all have in common their need for permanent but limited war to maintain their authority.

Permanent war is necessary because they cannot afford to give up the ruling Party's need to control society and hence control each individual's existence. Limited warfare is necessary because if the fighting occurs anywhere but in the Third World (Disputed Territories) it might upset the delicate balance between the three superpowers and hence lead to instability.

Any student of Modern History will see obvious parallels in our recent past in the delicate balance between the Americans, the U.S.S.R. and the Chinese as super powers and their influence on the disputes and wars in Africa and South America. Think back to the word 'Orwellian' and this certainly makes it applicable to our experiences today.

Double Think as a Means of Controlling Human Experiences

This concept is central to the control the Party has established and its means of continuing control over the people. The whole structure of this society is geared to a wartime economy.

This has two advantages in controlling the population. There is an "external enemy" who provides a focus for the fears of the people and hence a method of their control. Secondly living conditions can be blamed on the need to provide for the war and hence living conditions being poor can be the best state possible because without it their might be internal dissension. Seen from this perspective it is clear then that WAR IS PEACE is a necessary slogan to ensure continued social stability.

In much the same way the second major tenet of Oceania is FREEEDOM IS SLAVERY. Freedom of action is seen as a danger to the state and accepted as a valid means of social control. There are obvious parallels Orwell draws here between the demands of the Soviet government on its people to give up individual freedoms for the good of the state. This total acceptance of the will of the state has the seeds of the third slogan of the Party that is of course that IGNORANCE IS STRENGTH.

Here the concept of being like the little children of the state is carefully controlled. It is the need to give up intellectual individualism, which provides for Orwell a particularly heinous condition in this relationship between the society and the individual.

It is understood that in this society the Party has all wisdom so that the individual does not need to question or indeed think anything other than that which the Party wants them to think. All independent thought is dangerous to the Party because it will inevitably lead to a questioning of some or all aspects of the Party structure.

This is then the basis for the need of Party control: the individuality of the members of a society is diametrically opposed to the concept of a society where all the individuals accept that the "common good" is paramount.

Tensions within Society

It is accepted by the majority at the end of the Twentieth Century that a dynamic tension between elements of society is essential to ensure the growth of a society. It is the constant questioning of ideas and structure within a dynamic society which ensures not only its survival but also its adaptation to internal and external forces.

In Orwell's society the external tension which provides a social cohesion is the continuing war. The Two Minutes Hate period is a valuable means of social control as well as a relief valve for the dynamics of hate. The Party recognises that the populace need a focus of hate for their buried hatred of their condition and hence provide a ready focus for the tensions of the masses.

The society is encouraged to respond emotionally and not intellectually to their situation. As much as Big Brother is the focus of their adoration it is towards the enemy that an equal amount of hate is released and relieves the dynamic of the society.

There is a further traitor who is seen, in some ways, as being more dangerous to the state than the known enemies of Eurasia or Eastasia. The significance of this character to the society is that he and his group are seen to be the focus for those who question the state. They question the necessity of war. The book written by **Emmanuel Goldstein** has an historical perspective and calls for an examination of the facts and has an intellectual argument. All this is an undeniable attraction to 'subversives' who question the state.

Emmanuel Goldstein questions whether constant war is beneficial or necessary and no doubt he is a reference to the holocaust in

Germany; Emmanuel Goldstein is chosen as a name for a subversive as Jews were accused of economic and social subversion by the totalitarian Nazi Party. Also the name Emmanuel is another name for the Jewish Messiah who was to lead them to freedom from tyranny. This is possibly modelled on Leon Trotsky who was exiled from the USSR then murdered as a result of a political disagreement with Stalin.

It is in this framework that Winston becomes obsessed with the need to discover the nature of 'truth'.

Winston knows that whatever the Party states today, as being true is true but that whatever the Party states as being true will be true and will always have been true. The absolute power for forming the 'truth' of existence, of controlling history and hence both the present and the future is what provides a sound basis for controlling the society and limiting social dissent. There can be no experiences outside state control.

The totalitarian state Orwell describes controls the intellectual and emotional environment of its citizens. Not only is there a lack of freedom of speech but the freedom of thought has been taken away from them. It is against this background that Winston's clumsy attempt to search for his own identity and actually write his ideas down reveals to the reader the suspense of the novel; it provides the impetus for the discovery of the protagonist's journey in to the relationship between the state and the individual.

Religion (Spirituality) as a Human Experience

The Party is both Church and State and Big Brother as a figure steps in to symbolise the power of "good". He is a figure to be venerated and worshipped. The original revolutionaries of Ingsoc are long dead, probably in all the purges of the sixties but Big Brother, who is the embodiment of the Party, is immortal and cannot die.

"Of course he exists. Big Brother is the embodiment of the Party. Will he ever die? Of course not. How could he die?"

The role of Emmanuel Goldstein is the Lucifer to Big Brother's existence as "God". It is essential that there is a hated symbol which is ready to ensnare the unwary Party member for if there was no evil how could the Party be all that is good?

"an object of hostility more constant than either Eurasia or Eastasia ."

O'Brien says, "God is power". This statement reflects accurately the main theme of the novel: power is supreme.

The Weakness of the Proles

At first glance it appears that Orwell neglects the Proles altogether in his novel other than as a background for the workings and machinations of the Party. If the population of Oceania is 85% Prole i.e. 275 million with only 6 million Inner Party members and 40 million Outer Party members why are there experiences not considered in more detail? That number is surely impressive. Is it because their experiences are considered unworthy or irrelevant?

Even Emmanuel Goldstein's revolutionary book says about the Proles that they are "too much crushed by drudgery" to be a problem to the Party. O'Brien says of them, "They are helpless, like animals. Humanity is the Party. The others are outside and irrelevant."

However there is a strong case for the fact that Orwell may have wanted to stimulate the reader into action by his portrayal of what are essentially us — the readers — as being powerless and ineffectual. Orwell's most despondent message here may well reflect the author's wish to promote resistance by the depiction of the failure of the Proles — the masses — to be heard.

It was a stylistic device of Orwell's that was employed not only in this novel but also in *Animal Farm*. It has the intention of galvanising public opinion by examining not necessarily what is but a worst-case scenario for the human condition. What do you think? Has Orwell made you consider your experiences in a new light? How do you see the role of the proles both in the novel and in societies in general?

Is the novel a criticism of Communism?

Undoubtedly this novel has been used by anti-communist literature to emphasise Orwell's distaste for the Communist ideal but this is not the true representation of Orwell's writing. He was embarrassed in his own lifetime by some United States Republican newspapers which he saw as attempting to manipulate his message. Orwell maintained that "The real danger lies in the acceptance of a totalitarian outlook by intellectuals of all colours."

Orwell's true loathing was for the attempt to manipulate and control the thought of the populace by all the machinery of a state, whether it was capitalist or socialist/communist. He saw the only possible alternative for his vision of a way forward as being an end to the arms race.

"The only way I can imagine to avoid nuclear war or a spiralling arms race, either of which would spell an end to democracy, is by generating a spectacle of a community where people are relatively free and happy and where the main motive of life is not the pursuit of money or power."

More recently we have seen a rise in more nationalistic and insular thinking which for some is seen as increasing authoritarianism. Whatever you think the relevance of the text to human experiences is strong both in the narrative experience and in its more philosophical context.

Julia and her Human Experiences

Julia may well be the symbol for hope that Orwell inserts into the novel to allude to the continuing resistance to totalitarianism inherent in humanity. Julia is perhaps the great hope of change, as her relationship with Smith is representative of the need for the "worker" to form an alliance with the "middle class".

Julia an Outer Party member can be seen as a potential metaphor for the Proles. She is a 26 year old mechanic assigned to a novel writing machine but her sexual affair heals Winston who stops drinking, coughing. His ulcer subsides and he no longer finds life "intolerable".

Even though they both know their love will bring retribution they nevertheless expect their love to survive. Julia mistakenly says, "That's one thing they can't do. They can't get inside you."

The tragedy is the Ministry of Love does shatter them and extinguishes their love for each other so that when they meet again there is no spark.

Does this mean that there is no hope? Perhaps. Not because it is the rebellion of those who cannot be expected to rebel which is important. The proles are ignored and are merely bent on having a good time. Like them Julia is bored by politics, both revolutionary as well as official; this rebellion of hers which should not occur yet does is the strongest statement for the hidden masses.

Orwell's statement about the Proles contains a strong belief in their yet unachieved potential and is one of the major paradoxes of the novel. "Until they become conscious the proles will never rebel, and until after they have rebelled they cannot become conscious."

It is the alliance between the intelligencia in the middle class and the workers which is the real danger to a totalitarian regime.

Sex and Human Experiences

The society created in *Nineteen Eighty-Four* is not totally based on a reflection on communism but is a reflection on the authoritarianism inherent in all totalitarian regimes. When Orwell was writing in-between *Animal Farm* and *Nineteen Eighty-Four* about how the psychology of mass movements worked, he coined a phrase "power worship".

For Orwell this was a form of authoritarianism which was imbued with sexual sadism: a form of attraction which filled a deep yearning to have a dominant leader who would be able to take control of the actions of the population; someone who was an attractive or desirable leader who would make it attractive to give up one's personal liberties. It is the process of coercion and fear and the consent to accept tyranny which provided the basis for much of 1984's examination of the sexual tension within the novel as well as the attractiveness of giving up ones freedom to the Party.

Allied to the use of sexual feelings is the oppression of sexual activity by the party. This libidinal energy is to be freed to build up the hysteria and hatred against the enemies of the Party.

Sex is central to human experiences and part of one of our strong drives — i.e. to reproduce. The Party attempts to take this away. We can see how strong the drive is and its effect as it does change Winston significantly and makes Julia divert from acceptable behaviour. Think about how the sexual tensions are resolved by the Party and the impact of these not being released. How do you see the role of sex in the novel? Consider how significant it is to human experiences and the central role it plays here.

LANGUAGE

Orwell writes in an essay called 'Why I Write' in *Essays*,

> 'What I have most wanted to do throughout the past ten years is to make political writing into an art. My starting point is always a feeling of partisanship, a sense of injustice. When I sit down to write a book, I do not say to myself, 'I am going to produce a work of art.' I write it because there is some lie that I want to expose, some fact to which I want to draw attention, and my initial concern is to get a hearing. But I could not do the work of writing a book, or even a long magazine article, if it were not also an aesthetic experience.'

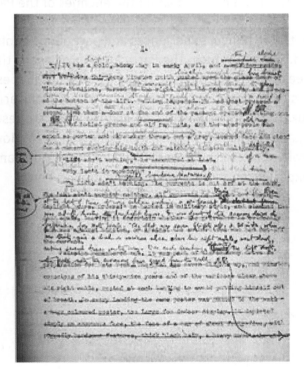

Orwell's writing has often been accused of being simplistic but we can see form the extensive revisions of the draft page shown here that he was considered and detailed in his work. Orwell always ensured his ideas were paramount and that they were available to all readers of his work. This is one of the keys to his success.

The most obvious commentary on the use of language in the novel is in the reduction of the number of words and therefore thoughts available to the people. It is the corruption of the true form of language to communicate feelings, ideas and opinions that marks the use of language to control the individual in this future society.

Although there is physical coercion it is the corruption and distortion of truth and thought which is the most terrifying aspect of Orwell's vision. The Ministry of Truth whose sole purpose is to distort and manipulate truth and The Ministry of Love, which uses torture to brainwash, are all valid examples of how language frames the thoughts of the individual.

We have previously discussed the corruption of language favoured by the Party but cannot leave any discussion of 1984 before mentioning the satirical nature of the text. Satire is the use of humour, irony, exaggeration or ridicule to expose the flaws and issues in society. Of course the satirical thrust of the novel is against the centralised state and we see much exaggeration and pathos. We can see the satirical bent of Orwell's work in doublethink, the erasing of the past, loss of individuality, the names of the ministries and the ironic slogans such as WAR IS PEACE which are also oxymorons. An oxymoron is a contradictory statement which contains a truth. In the case of our example war with a foreign nation such as Eastasia keeps people at home peaceful as they have a war to worry about.

Specific language techniques used by Orwell have been discussed in the commentary and other specific areas in the text and you should read this carefully with Orwell's purpose in mind. We have listed some quotes on the following pages which are linked to human experiences and the information discussed in these themes.

MEMORABLE QUOTES

Quote:

"BIG BROTHER IS WATCHING YOU"

PART 1, CHAPTER 1

Quote:

"WAR IS PEACE
FREEDOM IS SLAVERY
IGNORANCE IS STRENGTH."

PART 1, CHAPTER 1

Quote:

"one of those completely unquestioning, devoted drudges on whom, more even than on the Thought Police, the stability of the Party depended."

PART 1, CHAPTER 2

Quote:

"We shall meet in the place where there is no darkness."

PART 1, CHAPTER 2

Quote:

"'Who controls the past', ran the Party slogan, 'controls the future: who controls the present controls the past.'"

Part 1, Chapter 3

Quote:

"She had not a thought in her head that was not a slogan, and there was no imbecility, absolutely none, that she was not capable of swallowing if the Party handed it out to her."

Part 1, Chapter 6

Quote:

"Sexual intercourse was to be looked on as a slightly disgusting minor operation, like having an enema."

Part 1, Chapter 6

Quote:

"Heavy physical work, the care of home and children, petty quarrels with neighbors, films, football, beer, and, above all, gambling filled up the horizon of their minds."

Part 1, Chapter 7

Quote:

"*If there is hope*, wrote Winston, *it lies in the proles.*"

Part 1, Chapter 7

Quote:

"*Until they become conscious they will never rebel, and until after they have rebelled they cannot become conscious.*"

Part 1, Chapter 7

Quote:

"a nation of warriors and fanatics, marching forward in perfect unity, all thinking the same thoughts and shouting the same slogans, perpetually working, fighting, triumphing, persecuting — three hundred million people all with the same face."

Part 1, Chapter 7

Quote:

"He wondered, as he had many times wondered before, whether he himself was a lunatic. Perhaps a lunatic was simply a minority of one...But the thought of being a lunatic did not greatly trouble him: the horror was that he might also be wrong."

Part 1, Chapter 7.

Quote:

"Not merely the validity of experience, but the very existence of external reality, was tacitly denied by their philosophy...If both the past and the external world exist only in the mind, and if the mind itself is controllable-what then?"

Part 1, Chapter 7.

Quote:

"Freedom is the freedom to say that two plus two make four. If that is granted, all else follows."

Part 1, Chapter 7

Quote:

"At the sight of the words *I love you* the desire to stay alive had welled up in him, and the taking of minor risks suddenly seemed stupid."

Part 2, Chapter 1

Quote:

"Not merely the love of one person, but the animal instinct, the simple undifferentiated desire: that was the force that would tear the Party to pieces."

Part 2, Chapter 2, pg. 127

Quote:

"What was more important was that sexual privation induced hysteria, which was desirable because it could be transformed into war fever and leader worship."

Part 2, Chapter 3

Quote:

"from the moment of declaring war on the Party it was better to think of yourself as a corpse. 'We are the dead,' he said."

Part 2, Chapter 3

Quote:

"So long as they were actually in this room, they both felt, no harm could come to them."

Part 2, Chapter 5

Quote:

"she only questioned the teachings of the Party when they in some way touched upon her own life. Often she was ready to accept the official mythology, simply because the difference between truth and falsehood did not seem important to her."

Part 2, Chapter 5

Quote:

"He had the sensation of stepping into the dampness of a grave, and it was not much better because he had always known that the grave was there and waiting for him."

Part 2, Chapter 6

Quote:

"The terrible thing that the Party had done was to persuade you that mere impulses, mere feelings, were of no account, while at the same time robbing you of all power over the material world."

Part 2, Chapter 7

Quote:

"It's the one thing they can't do. They can make you say anything — *anything* — but they can't make you believe it. They can't get inside you."

Part 2, Chapter 7

Quote:

"You will work for a while, you will be caught, you will confess, and then you will die... There is no possibility that any perceptible change will happen within our own lifetime. We are the dead."

Part 2, Chapter 8

Quote:

"The primary aim of modern warfare (in accordance with the principles of *doublethink*, this aim is simultaneously recognised and not recognised by the directing brains of the Inner Party) is to use up the products of the machine without raising the general standard of living."

Part 2, Chapter 9

Quote:

"If the machine were used deliberately for that end, hunger, overwork, dirt, illiteracy, and disease could be eliminated within a few generations."

Part 2, Chapter 9

Quote:

"It was the product of a mind similar to his own, but enormously more powerful, more systematic, less fear-ridden. The best books, he perceived, are those that tell you what you know already."

Part 2, Chapter 9

Quote:

"the essential act of the Party is to use conscious deception while retaining the firmness of purpose that goes with complete honesty."

Part 2, Chapter 9

Quote:

"everywhere stood the same solid unconquerable figure, made monstrous by work and childbearing, toiling from birth to death and still singing."

Part 2, Chapter 10

Quote:

"The old feeling, that at bottom it did not matter whether O'Brien was a friend or an enemy, had come back. O'Brien was a person who could be talked to... O'Brien had tortured him to the edge of lunacy, and in a little while, it was certain, he would send him to his death. It made no difference."

Part 3, Chapter 2

Quote:

"He was the tormentor, he was the protector, he was the inquisitor, he was the friend".

Part 3, Chapter 2.

Quote:

"He had the air of a doctor, a teacher, even a priest, anxious to explain and persuade rather than to punish".

Part 3, Chapter 2.

Quote:

"You have known it for years, though you have fought against the knowledge. You are mentally deranged. You suffer from a defective memory...you are clinging on to your disease under the impression that it is a virtue."

Part 3, Chapter 2.

Quote:

"You would not make the act of submission which is the price of sanity. You preferred to be a lunatic, a minority of one...Whatever the Party holds to be the truth, *is* truth."

Part 3, Chapter 2.

Quote:

"'Do you remember writing in your diary,' he said, 'that it did not matter whether I was a friend or an enemy, since I was at least a person who understood you and could be talked to? You were right. I enjoy talking to you. Your mind appeals to me. It resembles my own mind except that you happen to be insane.'"

Part 3, Chapter 2

Quote:

"What can you do, thought Winston, against the lunatic who is more intelligent than yourself, who gives your arguments a fair hearing and then simply persists in his lunacy?"

Part 3, Chapter3.

Quote:

"The Party seeks power entirely for its own sake. We are not interested in the good of others, we are interested solely in power. Not wealth or luxury or long life or happiness: only power, pure power." 3,3

Quote:

"One does not establish a dictatorship in order to safeguard a revolution; one makes the revolution in order to establish the dictatorship".

Quote:

"We control matter because we control the mind. Reality is inside the skull."

Part 3, Chapter 3.

Quote:

"Unless he is suffering, how can you be sure that he is obeying your will and not his own? Power is inflicting pain and humiliation. Power is in tearing human minds to pieces and putting them back together again in new shapes of your own choosing".

Quote:

"The old civiliations claimed that they were founded on love and justice. Ours is founded upon hatred. In our world there will be no emotions except fear, rage , triumph and self-abasement."

Quote:

"If you want a picture of the future, imagine a boot stamping on a human face — for ever."

Quote:

"You are imagining that there is something called human nature which will be outraged by what we do and will turn against us. But we create human nature."

Quote:

"To die hating them, that was freedom."

Quote:

"For the first time he perceived that if you want to keep a secret you must also hide it from yourself."

Part 3, Chapter 4

Quote:

"There were things, your own acts, from which you could not recover. Something was killed in your breast; burnt out, cauterised out."

Part 3, Chapter 6

Quote:

"But it was all right, everything was all right, the struggle was finished. He had won the victory over himself. He loved Big Brother."

Part 3, Chapter 6

Quote:

"The purpose of Newspeak was not only to provide a medium of expression for the world-view and mental habits proper to the devotees of Ingsoc, but to make all other modes of thought impossible."

Appendix

SUGGESTED READING

- Atkins, John. *George Orwell*. London: John Calder Limited, 1954.
- Calder, Jenni. *Huxley and Orwell: Brave New World and Nineteen Eighty-Four*. London: Edward Arnold Ltd, 1976.
- Heller, Joseph. *Now and Then: From Coney Island to Here*. New York: Alfred A. Knopf, Inc., 1998.
- Orwell, George. *Collected Essays*. London: Secker and Warburg, 1961.
- Oxley, B.T. *George Orwell*. London: Evans Brothers Limited, 1976.
- Smith, D. Mosher, M. *Orwell for Beginners*. London: Writers and Readers Publishing Co-operative, 1984.
- Steinhoff, William. *The Road to 1984*. London: Weidenfeld and Nicolson, 1957.

THE ESSAY

The essay consists of the basic form of an introduction, body paragraphs and conclusion. The esssay has been the subject of numerous texts and you should have the basic form well in hand. As teachers, the point we would emphasise would be to link the paragraphs both to each other and back to your argument (which should directly respond to the question). Of course, ensure your argument is logical and sustained.

Make sure you use specific examples and that your quotes are accurate. To ensure that you respond to the question, make sure you plan carefully and are sure what relevant point each paragraph is making. It is solid technique to actually 'tie up' each point by explicitly coming back to the question.

When composing an essay the basic conventions of the form are:

- State your argument, outline the points to be addressed and perhaps have a brief definition.

A solid structure for each paragraph is:
- Topic sentence (*the main idea and its link to the previous paragraph/ argument*)
- Explanation/ discussion of the point including links between texts if applicable.
- Detailed evidence (*Close textual reference – quotes, incidents and technique discussion.*)
- Tie up by restating the point's relevance to argument/ question

- Summary of points
- Final sentence that restates your argument

As well as this basic structure, you will need to focus on:

Audience – for the essay the audience must be considered formal unless specifically stated otherwise. Therefore, your language must reflect the audience. This gives you the opportunity to use the jargon and vocabulary that you have learnt in English. For the audience ensure your introduction is clear and has impact. Avoid slang or colloquial language including contractions (like 'doesn't', 'e.g.', 'etc.').

Purpose – the purpose of the essay is to answer the question given. The examiner evaluates how well you can make an argument and understand the module's issues and its text(s). An essay is solidly structured so its composer can analyse ideas. This is where you earn marks. It does not retell the story or state the obvious.

Communication – Take a few minutes to plan the essay. If you rush into your answer it is almost certain you will not make the most of the brief 40 minutes to show all you know about the question. More likely you will include irrelevant details that do not gain you marks but waste your precious time. Remember an essay is formal so **do not** do the following: story-tell, list and number points, misquote, use slang or colloquial language, be vague, use non-sentences or fail to address the question.

PLAN:

Don't even think about starting without one!

Introduce...

the texts you are using in the response

Argument: The human experience is affected by:
- Idea One
- Idea Two
- Idea Three

You need to let the marker know what texts you are discussing. You can start with a definition but it can come in the first paragraph of the body. You MUST state your argument in response to the question and the points you will cover as part of it. Wait until the end of the response to give it!

↓

Idea One – Aspect of human experience as outlined in the textual material, e.g. physical impact.

Idea Two – Another aspect of human experience as outlined in the textual material, e.g. psychological impact.
- explain the idea
- where and how is it shown in the prescribed text?
- where and how is it shown in related text 1?

Idea Three – People's sense of experience is affected by context and environment
- explain the idea
- where and how shown in the prescribed text?
- where and how shown in related text 1?

You can use the things you have learned to organise the essay. For each one, you say where you saw this in your prescribed text and where in related text(s).

Two or three ideas are usually enough as you can explore them in detail.

↓

- Summary of two key ideas
- Final sentence that restates your argument

Make sure your conclusion restates your argument. It does not have to be too long.

MODEL ESSAY OUTLINE

> To what extent are human experiences significant in the set text?
>
> From your studies respond to this question using your set text and at ONE piece of other textual material

This essay needs to be attacked in a manner that responds to the question and shows ALL your knowledge about the text. The question lends itself to a close study of George Orwell's *Nineteen Eighty-Four* as the text does show how the human experience is integral to life and how it shapes our other experiences and interaction with the world.

An introduction might be written:

> Human experiences are important in Orwell's novel *Nineteen Eighty-Four* and the two related texts Lawrence's film *Jindabyne* and Ed Sheeran's song *Castle on the Hill*. These texts show how human experiences are integral to human existence and bring more meaning to one's life. Life is about experiences that challenge us and define how we see the world. They shape our beliefs and attitudes and can be confronting at the same time. Without experiences our lives would be empty and meaningless.

Your essay should then follow the outlined plan and develop these ideas. This gives you the opportunity to link the texts and fully develop each of the ideas.

ANNOTATED RELATED MATERIAL: DIFFERENT STUDIES OF HUMAN EXPERIENCES

Jindabyne – Ray Lawrence

Jindabyne is an Australian film that captures a wide array of human experiences. It touches on the ideas mentioned in the introduction to this text in a number of detailed instances. We can begin by considering the following before beginning a detailed examination of the narrative.

The collective human experience:

- Aboriginality and the spiritual;
- The Fishermen and their code;
- The reaction of the townsfolk;
- Media response;
- Interaction with the natural world.

Individual Experience:

- An individual character's response to the body – choose one;
- The killer;
- Response to the revelations;
- Past experiences and how they impact on current experiences;
- Reaction to loss – emotional;
- Assumptions about life.

We can now look at the plot to help us understand each of these issues. *Jindabyne* begins with the sound of a radio being tuned and the Australian feel of the movie is immediate with the theme music for the ABC news. Lawrence emphasises the isolation by having the radio not tune in correctly for an unknown female character, forcing her to use the cassette player. With this unusual beginning we know that her experience is not going to be positive.

We then pan to the rocks slowly where Gregory, our killer, sits patiently in a truck with the engine running watching the road. We know he is prepared for this as he has binoculars. He sees an Aboriginal girl, Susan O'Connor, driving and she is the one fiddling with the radio. He chases her down and forces her to stop. He moves toward her as we see a long shot of how isolated they are. We see his face in her window looming above her and screaming about the electricity coming down from the mountains. This film is no murder mystery, as we know from the beginning that the murderer is Gregory the electrician. This is about the experiences of the other characters in the film and how they respond to current experiences.

The Kane family, Stewart, Claire and son Tom, is waking. Claire pretends to sleep, before waking suddenly and being affectionate with Tom. Stewart and Tom head out fishing. The scene doesn't feel quite right and there is some emotional tension between Stewart and Claire that is unspoken due to what they have experienced in the past. Claire had a complicated past when she was pregnant with Tom. When she finds she is pregnant again, she becomes emotional and slightly unstable.

As the film builds we see the complex pasts of the characters and their interactions in the confinement of the small town. The fishing trip is a break from this and extremely important in their lives.

We see some of the emotional instability in characters such as Caylin-Calandria, who with Tom, has some issues at school. Along with Caylin-Calandria, Claire and Jude also have issues but in a nicely framed shot of the three female characters, we see them conform as members of a close knit group. The sacrifice they make is similar to Gregory's but on a different scale. Note the connection here and how each one is to get back to order and societal norms. This is the collective experience for all the characters.

At the Kanes' home the tensions are obvious from their past experiences but they contain it for appearances' sake. Occasionally, the tension reaches breaking point and the experience strains the superficial approach. The tension builds at home and the fishing trip seems like a good opportunity to break the cycle.

When we see Gregory dump Susan O'Connor's body in the river, we know that the fishing and her death will interact.

The next morning, the fishermen head off for their one big trip of the year and the sign 'Gone fishing' is put in the garage window. We see Billy on the phone to Elissa and putting the sign the wrong way round in the window shows his immaturity. They have already said they are taking him away to make a man of him. The four men have a few beers on the way and talk as they travel through the landscape. They intend to give Billy the experience they think he needs as a 'man' — a cultural rite of passage.

The men arrive and the high-tension electricity wires punctuate the wilderness. They begin to hike toward the valley. It's a long walk in and the terrain is hilly and difficult. They stop on the way and again we see Billy's naivety when Stewart says 'Listen to that' meaning the silence but he can't, as he has his earphones in. It is part of the break in tension of the film that they commune with nature. This experiential break affects all the men. The episode represents a distinct human experience.

Stewart wanders down the river fishing and sees Susan's body caught in the rocks. Hesitantly, he wades out to it and turns it over saying 'Oh Jesus' repeatedly. He screams for the others to come as he drags the body to the bank. He is obviously upset, making the sign of the cross. Stewart tells Rocco to 'take her, for fuck's sake, take her' and their shock is obvious. They all stare at the body and Billy goes to run off but they stop him. The four men meet and decide to leave her in the water and tie her so she doesn't float away.

The presence of the body threatens to detract from the enjoyment of the fishing experience. The act of attempted isolation of the bad experience is expected to evoke only a mild response. They do not anticipate the stormy reaction it receives when they return to the community.

The men go on fishing, with Stewart getting the first big fish on an absolutely perfect day. The lure of the fish is strong, especially when they see the big one he has caught. They have a successful and enjoyable time, a positive experience. They get a photo of the catch and Billy holds up his fish in a typical hunter/gatherer pose. Capturing an experience this way is most enjoyable.

It is a photo that will come back to haunt them as things change back in the world. An unanticipated adverse reaction can be a horrific experience.

Stewart goes to check on the dead girl, rolling her over and getting debris off her face in a quite tender gesture. The next day they head back and report it. At the car Billy rings Elissa and says they found a body but 'caught the most amazing fish'. They are told by the police to wait and seem despondent their trip has been ruined. They organise their story as Stewart says they have 'to get their story straight'.

We cut to Gregory eating breakfast and he appears to be a normal, lonely man until he goes out to his shed where he has hidden Susan's car and this reminds us of the evil in him. Consider his experience and his motivations. How does he see his actions and the world?

The next day at the station the policeman tells the fishermen 'we don't step over bodies for our recreational pursuits' and 'the whole town's ashamed of you'. When they are told to 'piss off' from the station the press are waiting for them and Billy makes a comment. Carl is angry with the press but we can begin to see signs of distress within the whole group.

The experience they had so looked forward to has become a negative one and the tensions we saw before are exacerbated by the emotional and collective response to the murder. Claire soon becomes obsessed with the whole affair because of her own state. The newspaper the next day has the headline, 'Men fish over dead body' because Billy has talked. Billy is late to work and Stewart tells him they have to 'stick together on this'.

Susan's sister calls them 'animals' and raises the race question by asking if they would have left a white girl. The Aboriginal youths begin to attack and vandalise the property of the men in violent outbursts, including throwing a rock through Billy's van window and thus endangering his baby. They insult Carl at the caravan park and vandalise the garage.

The police aren't any help and the situation deteriorates. Jude tells the police they shouldn't be enforcing the 'political correctness' laws. The intervention of the sense of Aboriginality and race challenges the assumptions people have and how we see the world. The contrasting views are ingrained in the social structures and part of different collective experiences.

The Aboriginal people see the white people as 'interfering' and the group of fishermen begin to fight amongst themselves. Elissa says they shouldn't go to the bush at all as it's sacred. The group talk about the bush and Rocco punches Stewart for saying the Aborigines are superstitious. The experience of racial tension becomes ever-present and adds to the emotional responses to the experience.

We now head slowly to a resolution of the conflict brought about by the various experiences. Each is handled in a different manner by characters and you can explore one or two of the responses. To cycle back to the original murder, Claire is stalked by Gregory in his truck. He stops her but drives off after staring weirdly, an odd experience in itself.

Terry and Stewart talk and Stewart meets Rocco and Carl. He tells them Claire's left him 'again'. Rocco can't believe it and we cross cut to her looking out into the wilderness after he looks thoughtfully out the window. These different reactions to experiences mirror attitudes in life and reactions to emotional and intellectual conflict.

In conclusion, Lawrence takes us back to the healing power of nature in our human experiences when the Aboriginal people are having a ceremony. Gregory watches while Claire walks in. Again we see his truck as an omnipresent force in the film, almost an extension of him. An Aboriginal man tells Claire to 'piss off' from the ceremony after she says she has come to pay her 'respects' but he is told to leave her alone by an Auntie.

The smoke and tribal music symbolise the ceremonial nature of the setting and the camera pans around the scene and the bush. We see parts of the ceremony with chanting and clapping sticks. The camera moves in and out while other shots pan around the bush, giving us the full experience and Lawrence portrays this as a positive, healing experience.

Eventually Stewart, Tom, Carl, Jude and Rocco arrive to pay respects. Tom runs to his mother and Stewart goes over and says 'Sorry' but is rebuffed by the father who throws dirt on him and spits, refusing his apology. Then an Aboriginal girl tells a little about Susan's story and sings the last love song Susan wrote.

The camera pans around all the faces as they listen to the song and the ceremonial smoke wafts around. It seems to have some healing effect on everyone, as it is a meaningful experience which raises the idea of the spiritual experience in the text. The girl stops singing through emotion. 'Be gone' seems to symbolise in language the whole scenario for each character.

We see a long wide shot of the bush before fading back to Gregory waiting again in his car behind the rocks for another victim. It is quite a circular conclusion and it is an odd end when he crushes the fly. We don't quite know what to make of the whole experience and he seems to be the only character unchanged by the experiences in the film.

Poem: 'Inland' by John Kinsella

The poem captures the mood and ethos of the outback farming communities and deals with the human aspect more than some of the other poems in Kinsella's collection: *Peripheral Light*. This poem is one long restless thought that mimics memories and recollection while raising the current, topical issues that concern the poet. As usual with his poems Kinsella orientates the audience early with the word 'Inland' and then continues the poem without a full stop. The poem flows with the use of commas but Kinsella allows us to stop and think with the use of the colon, brackets and the hyphen. Look for these punctuation stops as you read as they emphasise a specific point or idea that resonates with the audience.

The first stanza gives us a foreshadowing of the events to follow with the warnings in the words 'storm', 'alert' and 'uncertain'. This ominous tone is reinforced by the word 'ghosts' and the implication of death which is constant in much of Kinsella's poetry. The next stanza deals with a more human element and we get the country feel with the bracketed gossip about McHenry's accident which shows the close knit community. Habits here are formed as part of survival and known to all as we see 'the old man plying the same track' and the families possibly heading to church on the Sunday morning.

The third stanza returns to the vagaries of nature. Kinsella repeats 'uncertain' with regard to the weather. Weather and the environment play a large role in farming communities and it is especially so at sowing and harvest. Despite the uncertainty and 'ashen' days which alter 'moods', the community returns to their habits and routines which shape their lives. The next stage returns to the road and the implication of a journey but a journey that is straight and in conflict with the cycles of the natural world. The path seems already marked and measured. It is 'straight and narrow', marked by a theodolite.

The final four lines of the poem are pure Kinsella, marking the transience of humanity on the landscape. We read

> 'it's a place of borrowed dreams
> where the marks of the spirit
> have been erased by dust –
> the restless topsoil'

The European farmers had 'borrowed dreams' for their own relationship with the land but this line also harks back to the indigenous Dreamtime when the land was created. The indigenous view that the land owns the people is also true for Kinsella. This sense of nobody owning the land is strong in his poetry. European impact on the land can be seen in the spirituality being removed by the dust—dust created by the poor farming techniques transferred from a different land. He finishes with the 'restless topsoil' as if the whole earth is moving in its own discontented journey, just as the people move.

The influence here of genuinely lost spirituality and connection with the land as we move directly on the 'high road' contrasts with the more flowing, 'restless' side of the natural world. This visual contrast is obvious but we can also discuss the contrast between habit and spirit. 'Inland' is a poem that uses the landscape to show the contrast between two views of the countryside.

DRAMA: Eugene O'Neil's *Desire Under the Elms*

O'Neill sets out to instruct how the house and elms should appear and the year is 1850. Note how he describes the 'enormous' elms as,

> 'exhausted women resting their sagging breasts and hands and hair on its roof, and when it rains their tears trickle down monotonously and rot on the shingles'

and how they dominate and 'rot'. It is important to read this both in terms of the play and in the context of American theatre. The description here shows O'Neill's genius at new design and original theatricality.

Part One: Scene One

The whole first page and a third are nearly all playwright notes that describe the farm, the house and the characters of Eben, Simeon and Peter. The first words of the play, 'God! Purty!' reflect the beauty of the land and how Eben perceives it. Eben is 'resentful and defensive' and feels 'trapped' on the farm.

His older half-brothers Simeon and Peter are 'more bounce and homelier in face, shrewder and more practical.' They all have worked hard on their father's farm over the years and have little feeling for their absent father. We learn that Simeon had a 'woman' who died and that Peter is excited by the prospect of 'gold in the West'. They all talk about how hard they've worked and hope that the father might 'die soon'. What we get from all this is that they are earthy and this is reflected in their bodies and clothes which are all dirt stained.

We also see here the difference between them as Eben sees gold in the pasture, not California, as they head in for a dinner of bacon in what seems a ritual they have performed many times before. Note that O'Neill calls for the use of the curtain at the end of the scene.

Scene Two

It is twilight and again we get detailed notes on the interior scene. Simeon tells Eben he should not wish their father dead and Eben replies he's not his son but, 'I'm Maw – every drop of blood!' He then blames the father, Ephraim Cabot, for killing his mother by working her to death but the others just say there was work to be done. O'Neill gets them to list the jobs and Eben comes back with 'vengeful passion' that, while they did nothing, he will see his mother gets 'rest and sleep in her grave!'

They then discuss Cabot's absence and how he just drove off in a buggy one day in a rush. Simeon says that when he went,

'He druv off in the buggy, all spick an' span, with the mare all breshed an' shiny, druv off clackin' his tongue an' wavin' his whip. I remember it quite well'

Eben mocks Simeon for not stopping him and the scene concludes with Eben leaving to see Minnie the town whore. We learn all the Cabot men have slept with her. Simeon and Peter say that Eben is just like 'Paw' and thinks of California. The final image is of Eben with his arms stretched to the sky talking about starts and sin, 'my sin's as purty as any one on 'em!', until he 'strides' to the village for Min.

Scene Three

It is 'pitch darkness' and Eben comes home with the news that Cabot has married a 'purty' thirty-five year old. He has heard this in the village and this effectively disinherits the boys. Simeon and Peter see California as their only option now. Eben tells the boys that they can have three hundred dollars each if they sign their share of the farm over to him. He can get the money as his mother told him,

> 'I know whar it's hid. I been waitin' – Maw told me. She knew whar it lay fur years, but she was waitin'....It's her'n – the money he hoarded from her farm an' hid from Maw. It's my money by rights now.'

They think about it and Eben tells them about his night with Min. He tells how he hates the new wife after the boys suggest he might sleep with her, just like Min, to get the old man back. Peter and Simeon say they'll do the deal and leave the farm. Both are bitter and vindictive about Cabot.

Scene Four

The setting is the same as Scene Two and the boys are discussing how they don't have to work now – it is all down to Eben who is jubilant as he thinks it will all be his. Peter and Simeon again reflect on how like his father he is, 'Like his Paw'. They also tell he isn't much of a milker but they soon talk about their leaving and how they'll miss some aspects of the farm.

Eben comes back in and says that the 'old mule an the bride' are coming. The two older boys begin to pack and sign Eben's papers as he gives them the money Cabot had hidden. They tell him they'll send him 'a lump o' gold for Christmas' and head into the yard feeling 'light' because of their newfound freedom.

Ephraim Cabot and Abbie Putnam then come in and O'Neill describes them in detail. Cabot is

> 'seventy-five, tall and gaunt, with great, wiry, concentrated power, but stoop shouldered by toil. His face is hard as if it were hewn from a boulder, yet there is a weakness in it'

but his face is weakened with petty pride. Abbie is

> 'thirty-five, buxom, full of vitality. Her round face is pretty but marred by its rather gross sensuality. There is strength and obstinacy in her jaw, a hard determination in her eyes, and about her whole personality.'

She also has a 'desperate quality'. Cabot shows Abbie the place and she says to him it's 'mine'. Then he sees the two boys not working. He introduces Abbie and she goes to look at 'her' house and they warn her Eben's inside.

Cabot tells them to get to work and they give him cheek, saying they are 'free' and heading to California. They 'whoop' it up and he says he'll have them chained up. They throw rocks at the house, smashing the window and head off singing. Abbie sticks her head out the window and says she likes the room but he is thinking of the stock and 'almost runs' to the barn.

Abbie then meets Eben in the kitchen and talks to him in 'seductive tones'. She says she doesn't want to be his 'Maw' but friends and he cusses her. She tells him of her troubled life and how Cabot gave her a chance to escape it. He calls her a 'harlot' and they argue over ownership of the farm. She has the upper hand in law and he leaves but the seeds of their growing attraction have been set.

Outside he and his father argue about life and work and he tells Eben 'Ye'll never be more'n half a man!' The scene ends with Abbie washing up and the faint notes of the song the boys were singing as they left.

Part Two: Scene One

Again O'Neill describes in detail the farmhouse setting. Two months have passed and it is a hot Sunday afternoon. Abbie in her best outfit is sitting on the porch and Eben comes out of the house also dressed in his best. They stalk each other, both attracted and repelled. As he walks away she 'gives a sneering, taunting chuckle' at him and they argue but the attraction is obvious. She says that nature will pull him to her but he says that she is married and he goes to leave her.

She accuses him of going to Min and she gets angry stating he'll never get the farm,

> 'Ye'll never live t' see the day when even a stinkin' weed on
> it 'll belong t' ye!'

He says he hates her and leaves as Cabot enters. She tells him Eben has been mocking him and twists the conversation to the inheritance of the farm. She tells him Eben lusts after her and as he angers she backs off in her accusations. Reassured, he says that she can have the farm if she bears the son she says she wants with him. He says that he'd 'do anythin' ye axed, I tell ye!' if she gave him a son and tells her to pray to God for it to happen.

Scene Two

It is about eight in the evening and here the bedrooms are highlighted, with Eben in one and Cabot with Abbie in the other. The two of them are talking about a son. They seem together, yet apart, as he tells her of his life on the farm and how God's hard. He both lost and gained on the way through, but the farm is his. He says he is pleased he found her, his 'Rose o' Sharon'. Abbie promises him that she will bear a son as he basically threatens her,

> 'Ye don't know nothin' – nor never will. If ye don't hev a son t' redeem ye...'

and he leaves to sleep in the barn with the cows 'whar it's restful'.

We then see Eben and Abbie restless and she leaves the room and goes to him. He 'submits' to her kisses then 'hurls' her away. Abbie says she'd make him 'happy' and she knows he wants her too much. She tells him to go down to the parlour and he is shocked as this is where his mother was 'laid out'. She leaves for the parlour and he wonders what's happening. The scene closes with a question to his dead mother, 'Maw! Whar are yew?' but we know that he wants her and will go to her.

Scene Three

The scene now shifts to the parlour which is described as a 'grim, repressed room like a tomb'. Abbie waits and Eben appears and he sits at her invitation. They talk about his Maw and how they hate Cabot. Abbie throws herself at him with 'wild passion' and he is caught up in the moment and thinks that it's his Maw wanting him to sleep with Abbie to get revenge on Cabot,

> I see it! I sees why. It's her vengeance on him – so's she
> kin rest quiet in her grave!

Abbie proclaims her love for him and he for her then they kiss 'in a fierce, bruising kiss' to close the scene.

Scene Four

A more bold and confident Eben leaves the house and Abbie opens the parlour window. She calls him over for a kiss and they talk a bit before Eben says his Maw can now rest. They split as Cabot comes out of the barn but are now obviously in love. Eben tells Cabot that his Maw is now at rest and Cabot says he rests best with the cows. Cabot is confused but the scene ends with him criticising Eben as 'Soft-headed' and a 'born fool' but, being a practical man, he heads for breakfast.

Part Three: Scene One

Time has passed to 'late spring the following year'. Eben is upstairs in emotional and psychological conflict while a party happens downstairs. Cabot has drunk too much and Abbie sits, pale and thin, in a rocking chair. There is a fiddler and Abbie begins the scene by asking for Eben and the guests 'titter' as most think the baby is Eben's, not Cabot's, which is true enough. They laugh and Cabot is angered by this and orders them to dance. The fiddler 'slyly' says they're waiting for Eben but Cabot mocks the boy and then ensues a bawdy conversation about his fertility,

> I got a lot in me – a hell of a lot – folks don't know on.
> Fiddle 'er up, durn ye! Give 'em somethin' t' dance t!'

The fiddler plays and they dance. Cabot joins in frantically and 'whoop(s)' it up. He exhausts the fiddler and pours whiskey. In the upstairs room Eben is looking at the baby. Abbie goes upstairs and Cabot leaves for outside, 'fresh air', as she has told him not to 'tech' her. The guests gossip after he goes and we see Eben and Abbie upstairs and she professes her love for him,

'Don't git feelin' low. I love ye, Eben. Kiss me.'

Cabot says he's going to rest in the barn. The scene concludes with the fiddler playing in celebration of 'the old skunk gittin' fooled!'

Scene Two

Eben is outside half an hour later and Cabot is coming back from the barn. Cabot tells him to get a woman inside and he might get a farm. Eben replies that this farm's his and Cabot mocks him. He tells her Abbie has been promised the farm for her son and Eben is angered thinking Abbie has tricked him.

Eben goes to kill her but Cabot is too strong for him and Abbie comes out to stop him choking Eben. Cabot tells him he's weak and goes inside to celebrate. Abbie tries to be tender with Eben but he rejects her and calls her a liar.

'Ye're nothin' but a stinkin' passel o' lies. Ye've been lyin' t' me every word ye spoke, day an' night, since we fust – done it. Ye've kept sayin' ye loved me....'

She says she loves him and tells him that the promise was made before they fell in love. He says he'll go to California.

They argue and he 'torturedly' says he wished the baby had never been born. Abbie is distraught and she says she'd kill the baby to prove her love for him. He says he won't listen to her but she calls after him that she can 'prove' she loves him and she 'kin do one thin' God does'. Abbie is desperate at the end of the scene.

Scene Three

It is now just before dawn and Eben is in the kitchen ready to leave. Abbie is near the cradle with 'her face full of terror'. She sobs but Cabot stirs and she goes to the kitchen and flings her arms around Eben, kissing him 'wildly'. She says 'I killed him' and he thinks she means Cabot but is horrified when she tells him it's the baby.

Eben states it was his baby and she says she loved it but loves him more. He is angered,

> 'Don't ye tech me! Ye're pizzen! How could ye – t' murder
> a pore little critter – Ye must've swapped yer soul t' hell!

and tells her that he is getting the Sheriff and heads, 'panting and sobbing' to town. She calls out to him that she loves him.

Scene Four

It is after dawn and Abbie is in the kitchen. Cabot wakes in his room and is concerned that he has woken late. He checks the baby and is proud it is quiet and asleep. He goes down to Abbie in the kitchen and she tells him the baby is dead. He runs to check and comes back down and asks 'why?'

In a rage she tells him it was Eben's son and that she loves Eben, not him. He blinks back a tear and then gets 'stony' so he can carry on and says he is going to get the Sheriff. Abbie tells him that Eben's already gone so that Cabot tells her he'll 'git t' wuk.' He then tells her he'd never have told and now he's going to be 'lonesomer'n ever!' Eben comes back and Cabot tells him to get off the farm.

Eben asks for her forgiveness and tells her he loves her. He says he realised he loved her at the Sheriff's and they have a chance to run away but Abbie says she'll take her punishment. Eben says he will share it with her and plans to tell the Sheriff they planned it together. They think they can stand it together and then Cabot comes back.

He goes into a long tirade and tells them how he's let the stock go and will burn the house down. He too plans to go to California but finds that Eben has gotten to his money first. Cabot says that this is a sign from God to him to stay and that 'God's hard an' lonesome!' At this point the Sheriff comes and Eben says he was involved with the baby's murder.

Cabot says 'Take 'em both' and leaves to get his stock. The sun is coming up and as they are led away Eben says the farm's 'Purty' and Abbie agrees. The Sheriff finishes the play with the line, 'It's a jim-dandy farm, no denyin'. Wish I owned it!'

OTHER RELATED TEXTS

Fiction / Non-fiction / Drama

- *Wonder* – R G Palacio
- *First they Killed My Father* – Luong Ung
- *The Graveyard Book* – Neil Gaiman
- *Looking for Alaska* – John Green
- *Eleanor and Park* by Rainbow Rowell
- *The Fault in Our Stars* – John Green
- *We All Fall Down* – Robert Cormier
- *The Old Man and the Sea* – Ernest Hemingway
- *The Fire Eaters* – David Almond
- *Ender's Game* – Orson Scott Card
- *Hatchet* – Gary Paulsen
- *Inside Black Australia* – Kevin Gilbert
- *Sapiens: A Brief History of Humankind* – Yuval Noah Harari
- *Peeling the Onion* – Wendy Orr
- *Raw* – Scott Monk
- *Six Degrees of Separation* – John Guare
- *The Book Thief* – Markus Zusak
- *When Dogs Cry* – Markus Zusak
- *Holes* – Louis Sachar
- *The Outsiders* – S.E. Hinton
- *Roll of Thunder, Hear My Cry* – Mildred D. Taylor
- *A Small Free Kiss in the Dark* – Glenda Millard
- *Monster* – Walter Dean Myers
- *Lord of the Flies* – William Golding
- *Jandamarra* – Steve Hawke
- *A Separate Peace* – John Knowles
- *A Monster Calls* – Patrick Ness
- *The Pigman* – Paul Zindel
- *The Invention of Hugo Cabret* – Brian Selznik

- *Emerald City* – David Williamson
- *Silent Spring* – Rachel Carson

Films and Television

- *The Human Experience* – Charles Kinnane
- *My Brilliant Career* – Gillian Armstrong
- *Broadchurch* – James Strong & Euros Lyn
- *Twinsters* – Samantha Futerman and Ryan Miyamoto
- *Be My Brother* – Genevieve Clay - Smith
- *What's Eating Gilbert Grape* – Lasse Hallstrom
- *Pleasantville* – Gary Ross
- *Eternal Sunshine of the Spotless Mind* – Michel Gondry
- *Taxi Driver* – Martin Scorsese
- *Tootsie* – Sydney Pollack
- *Back in Time for Dinner* – Kim Maddever
- *The Godfather* – Francis Ford Coppola
- *Friends* – David Crane and Marta Kaufmann
- *Dawson's Creek* – Kevin Williamson
- *Orange is the New Black* – Jenji Kohan
- *Boy Meets World* – Michael Jacobs and April Kelly

Website – quote on literature and the human experience

http://view2.fdu.edu/academics/university-college/school-of-humanities/
english-language-and-literature-program/

At its most fundamental level literature explores what it means to be a human being in this world and tries to describe what our human experience is like. As such, literature pushes us to confront the large human questions that have plagued humankind for centuries: issues of fate and free will, issues relating to our role in the universe, our relationship to God, and our relationships with others. Studying literature not only helps us to understand the complexity of these questions intellectually, but because of its very nature, it allows us to experience these tensions vicariously. Literature does not just tell us about human experience; it recreates it in a way we can feel and visualise. In other words, it calls for a total response from us—it stretches us beyond who we are.

First, literature can enhance our ability to relate to people. Because literature focuses on human relationships and self perception, it can broaden our own experience—to help us understand different kinds of people, different cultures, different problems—and, consequently, help us better understand our own relationships with others.

The study of literature also helps to foster an appreciation for beauty, symmetry, and order. This means more than the intuitive response of liking or disliking something we see or read or hear; it means a carefully thought-through response that will enhance appreciation—not destroy it.

Perhaps the most important skills that the study of literature teaches are analytic and synthetic skills. In learning to read carefully and analytically, we learn to ask hard questions both of the work and of ourselves. And as we seek to discover the relationships between the ideas and images we uncover in a work, our ultimate goal is to see the whole—to see how the parts work together to make the piece what it is. In grappling with the complex and difficult ideas contained in literature, we learn to accept the multiple dimensions and ambiguity that are so often present in life.

Finally, the study of literature will also help develop our writing abilities as we come to value the written word and understand its power to communicate.

Beyond all of these skills, however, it is not what literature can do for us as individuals as much as what it can do to us. Literature speaks to the whole person. Listen to it, says C. S. Lewis, and you will be changed.

Poetry

- 'Warren Pryor' – Alden Nowlan
- 'The Gardener' – Louis MacNeice
- 'The Improvers' – Colin Thiele

Songs

- *Be My Escape* – Relient K
- *Mandolin Wind* – Rod Stewart
- *Roxanne* – The Police
- *Wake Me Up When September Ends* – Green Day
- *Under Pressure* – Queen & David Bowie
- *Candle in the Wind* – Elton John
- *Empire State of Mind* – Alicia Keys
- *Gold Digger* – Kanye West
- *We Are Young* – Fun.
- *Centrefold* – J. Geils Band
- *It's Time* – Imagine Dragons
- *We Cry* – The Script
- *If I Were a Boy* – Beyoncé
- *Shake it Out* – Florence + the Machine
- *C'mon* – Panic! At the Disco & Fun.
- *I Don't Love You* – My Chemical Romance
- *Sing* – My Chemical Romance
- *1985* – Bowling for Soup
- *What About Me* – Shannon Noll
- *Sinner* – Jeremy Loops
- *7 Years* – Lucas Graham

- *Bitter Sweet Symphony* – The Verve
- *Ghost!* – Kid Kudi
- *Good Riddance (Time of Your Life)* – Green Day
- *Expectations* – Belle and Sebastian
- *After Hours* – We Are Scientists
- *Write About Love* – Belle and Sebastian
- *Trust Your Stomach* – Marching Band
- *Heaven Knows I'm Miserable Now* – The Smiths